Modern Enterprise Architecture

Using DevSecOps and Cloud-Native in Large Enterprises

Jeroen Mulder

Apress®

Modern Enterprise Architecture: Using DevSecOps and Cloud-Native in Large Enterprises

Jeroen Mulder
Emmen, The Netherlands

ISBN-13 (pbk): 978-1-4842-9065-1   ISBN-13 (electronic): 978-1-4842-9066-8
https://doi.org/10.1007/978-1-4842-9066-8

Managing Director, Apress Media LLC: Welmoed Spahr
Acquisitions Editor: Aditee Mirashi
Development Editor: James Markham
Coordinating Editor: Aditee Mirashi

Cover designed by eStudioCalamar

Cover image designed by Freepik (www.freepik.com)

Distributed to the book trade worldwide by Springer Science+Business Media New York, 1 New York Plaza, Suite 4600, New York, NY 10004-1562, USA. Phone 1-800-SPRINGER, fax (201) 348-4505, e-mail orders-ny@ springer-sbm.com, or visit www.springeronline.com. Apress Media, LLC is a California LLC and the sole member (owner) is Springer Science + Business Media Finance Inc (SSBM Finance Inc). SSBM Finance Inc is a **Delaware** corporation.

For information on translations, please e-mail booktranslations@springernature.com; for reprint, paperback, or audio rights, please e-mail bookpermissions@springernature.com.

Apress titles may be purchased in bulk for academic, corporate, or promotional use. eBook versions and licenses are also available for most titles. For more information, reference our Print and eBook Bulk Sales web page at http://www.apress.com/bulk-sales.

Any source code or other supplementary material referenced by the author in this book is available to readers on GitHub via the book's product page. For more detailed information, please visit http://www.apress.com/source-code.

Printed on acid-free paper

For the people with a growth mindset.

Table of Contents

About the Author

Jeroen Mulder (born 1970) started his career as a journalist, focusing on economy and technology. In 1999, he joined the Dutch IT company Origin that later became Atos Origin and AtoS. From that year onward, he trained himself to become an enterprise and business architect. Today, he is a principal consultant and enterprise architect with the Japanese IT services company Fujitsu. Jeroen has previously written several books about multi-cloud and DevOps.

About the Technical Reviewer

 **Pedro Valido** is Head of Transformation for Cloud, Data, and DX for Western Europe at Fujitsu, one of the top global technology service providers. He is also the managing partner of White Fountain, a business agility and transformation consultancy, and 4theChange, an international change management practice. He is coordinator and teaching assistant at Universidade Europeia in Lisbon, Portugal. Pedro received his diploma from Glion Institute of Higher Education, Switzerland, and also passed several international certifications in behavioral change, the last one on the sales methodology Challenger from Gartner. He also recently completed his certification as a SAFe 5 Agilist.

Acknowledgments

First, I have to thank my wife and my daughters for granting me all this time that I spent in my little home office, burying myself in piles of books, listening to podcasts, viewing webinars, talking long hours to a lot of people that I admire in the field of enterprise architecture and change management, and, of course, writing.

Writing takes stamina. Not only of the writer, but even more so from his or her surrounding. So, this is for my wife Judith and my girls Rosalie and Noa. You make me so very proud as a husband and a father.

Can't promise that this will be my last book, though. A man's got to do what an architect needs to do.

A big thank you goes to friend, colleague, and master of change Pedro Valido who has reviewed this work in a very thorough manner. With fair criticism and an eye for the smallest details, he absolutely improved the work by a zillion percent.

Lastly, I want to thank Aditee Mirashi of Apress for reaching out to me and persuading me to write this book.

Foreword

How do you link market, customer, business, and enterprise architecture in an aligned plan?

Let me start with the obvious, the why of this book: enterprises need to transform if they want to survive and thrive in a digital, agile, and evolving world. The also obvious question is how and where to start. This book gave me great insights on these topics.

As I read through this book, I was able to realize there is much more to business and digital transformation than meets the eye. I have changed my own mindset on the approach with the structure of thought, processes, and frameworks that the complexity of the new and different challenges require across customer, business strategy, culture, ways of working, teaming up, and execution, to name a few. I have progressively shifted in my thinking from "delayed perfection" to "continuous improvement," from "A to B mentality" to "ever evolving and adaptable," from "blame" to "continuous feedback."

As a fellow transformation, business agility, and change practitioner, make no mistake: digital transformation is hard. Very hard. And complex. It touches all parts of the enterprise (leaders, people at all "levels," processes, business architecture, and technology), as the challenges have never been so complex and interdependent. It's not about technology, it's about overall transformation (and technology is one of the building blocks).

It will take a complete, integrated, agile, top-down, bottom-up team and community-based change approach to transition to an agile and market-ready enterprise. All this to deliver tangible business value sooner rather than later, more frequently while mobilizing the workforce around it. This is the real challenge to which this book provides the answer.

If you are starting or continuing this journey in your own present or future role, you will learn (as I have) a great deal on the main processes and frameworks linked to this transformation journey, and more importantly it will help you fill the (not so obvious) "missing link(s)" between business and enterprise architecture, the critical aspects on where to start (or continue), coupled with a clear view of the challenges to enable this vision:

- Why transform?

- Where we stand today?

- What to transform into?

- The challenges and roadmap: Where to start, the new mindset (or should I say culture?), the critical success factors of the enterprise architecture, the new skill set of the enterprise architect.

In the midst of all this, among other identified changes, the role of the enterprise architect – the true center stage role of this transformation – has evolved.

Spoiler alert: Apart from all the renewed strategic aspects (customer, business, and enterprise architecture), soft skills (also known as life skills or power skills) play a major role in enabling the success of the enterprise architect, enabler of agile working, CI/CD, DevSecOps, and other practices for success.

I strongly believe these skills are the "magic glue" that enables the enterprise to go from a hierarchical structure to a living organism in strategy implementation. Jeroen Mulder talks a lot about this living organism on the part of team formation as the most critical aspect of execution. And I couldn't agree more, as someone who supports, enables, and helps transform a regional workforce for several years (and struggles with the daily challenges associated).

I am now using this book as a reference to help me engage better at all levels of the organization and asking others (or myself) the "difficult" (yet unavoidable) questions: How is our customer transforming, what is our go to market, what are our customers' challenges, how do we link business goals to enterprise architecture, what solutions do we need to provide to create business value, how do we understand the current IT estate and adapt, what capability do we need to have (or build), what is our roadmap, how do we form taskforces and team up across countries, service lines, business lines, and influence (rather than dictate) outcomes? Last but not least, finding the right balance between top-down and bottom-up approaches.

I hope you will enjoy reading this book as much as I have. No matter the outcome, brace yourself, you're in for a ride. A difficult, mind-shifting, yet necessary ride for most organizational practitioners, regardless of the level of technical knowledge.

Pedro Valido

November 2022

Introduction

My career in IT started in 1999, when I joined the Dutch IT company Origin. Frankly, I knew not a lot about IT, let alone architecture. What I did know was that I wanted to learn – as much as I could. Luckily, the motto of the company was "sharing the power of knowledge," so it wasn't hard to find people who were more than willing to teach me "tech."

After a few years, I came to the discovery that technology for the sake of technology was worthless to businesses. There had to be a strong connection between business and technology. Enterprise architecture provided that connection. The next discovery was that enterprise architecture itself was also, in many cases, focused on enabling technology, especially when cloud and digital transformation started entering the scene. Cloud and digital have been and will be major disruptors for almost every business, with a huge impact to organizations and the people in these organizations.

That insight has been the driver for this book. This book is absolutely about tech, but more so about how technology is driving the change of enterprises. They have to evolve and have to get faster in development, more agile, and closer to their customers, continuously capturing the voice of their customers. Technology is only a small part of this whole process. Enterprises will change to the core, including the organization of the enterprise itself, almost constantly changing. That is what this book is about.

Something that floats has little friction, but just enough friction in order not to sink. A floating object just has enough mass to float but is free to move in every direction and to gain speed. The enterprise architect is the sailor and the navigator on this new ship that has set course to a cloud-born North Star.

Going digital is a rough sea for earth-born companies, which most enterprises are. We need more sailors.

CHAPTER 1

Why Businesses Need Enterprise Architecture

In this first chapter, I will explain why any business in any industry needs enterprise architecture (EA). You will learn what enterprise architecture is by studying different frameworks such as The Open Group Architecture Framework (TOGAF) and Zachman. You will also discover why these are relevant to the business, but also why it's necessary to develop new perspectives to enterprise architecture because of the changing, digital ecosystem where enterprises find themselves today. We will take a first look at emergent architectures, North Stars, and methodologies such as Quality Function Deployment (QFD) and Open Agile Architecture (O-AA). Spoiler alert: Enterprise architecture is not about technology in the first place.

Introduction to Enterprise Architecture

Enterprise architecture (EA) in many organizations is still a big unknown, which is logical if you realize that EA is a relatively "new kid on the block." The profession itself originates somewhere from the 1980s but didn't get much traction up until the late 1990s and beginning of the new millennium – the era where enterprises really started implementing new, big technology and exploring the possibilities of digitalization.

Suddenly, it became important to have businesses aligned with the growth and implementation of information technology. It became core business – in fact quite an antipattern if you realize that many enterprises during the 1990s and first decennium of the new millennium decided to outsource their IT since it was not core business. That has changed completely, leaving a very important role for the enterprise architect.

EA became the driver for business change, using that information technology especially to understand and use data. Business data became available in many formats and in vast quantities, almost overloading the enterprise with information. Management

1

© Jeroen Mulder 2023
J. Mulder, *Modern Enterprise Architecture*, https://doi.org/10.1007/978-1-4842-9066-8_1

needed to find ways to make sense of that data and how it could be used to drive the business, to grow markets, and to increase revenues and profits. Data had to be analyzed to see if businesses were on track or if customers were demanding new products or services. Who were these customers? Why did they want new products? Where were these customers located? Where could new customers be found and how could a company increase market share? Was a company ready to scale? Were systems prepared to scale?

In short, enterprises needed to be ready for constant change in their portfolio. If a company had the data and they knew what the markets required, the next challenge was how to develop and deliver those new products and services in a timely, coherent way. This is where EA came to the rescue.

But what *is* EA really?

Let's start with a very simple explanation of EA. It's the sum of strategy, business, and technology as shown in Figure 1-1. Basically, you could say that EA helps you organize and focus on the business goals, supported by technology.

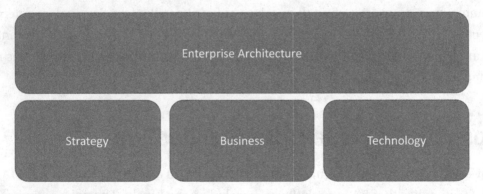

Figure 1-1. *The three pillars of enterprise architecture*

To be very clear, yes, it's also about technology, but not only about technology. EA is putting these three pillars together in a holistic, overarching model that drives the enterprise. It takes the strategic direction of the enterprise as the starting point, defines the business practices that support the strategy, identifies the information and data flows within the businesses, and next decides what technology fits best to enable the fulfillment of the business and thus bring value to the entire enterprise. EA helps to plan the resources that are required to design and build solutions that bring this value.

Information technology (IT) has become one of the critical resources, but as stated, EA must have a holistic view, so there are more components that define the enterprise architecture of the enterprise, as shown in Figure 1-2.

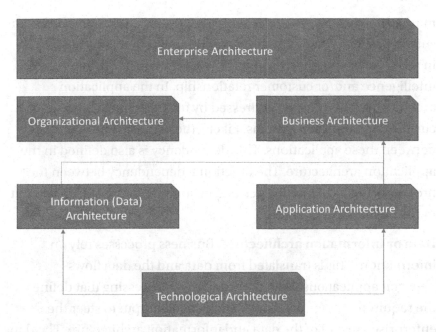

Figure 1-2. *The components of EA*

Let's discuss the different architectural components:

- **Organizational architecture**: The "blueprint" on how the enterprise is structured. It addresses where people sit in the organization and what their tasks are in alignment with the strategy of the organization. It helps to make organizational architecture visible, for example, by using organizational charts and functional organigrams.

- **Business architecture**: This architecture defines the purpose of the enterprise, the different functions, and critical processes that an enterprise needs to operate the business.

- **Application architecture**: The enterprise will have applications to run the business. The application architecture lays out the patterns to build and operate the applications. It also defines the integration between applications in the enterprise's application landscape. The application architecture should follow the business architecture since applications enable the enterprise to operate the business. For example, the enterprise likely has a need to have a clear overview of its market and customers, comprehensively visualized and presented to end users in the form of dashboards with parameters such as market insights, net promoter score (NPS), and customer satisfaction surveys (CSAT). That's a business requirement that is addressed in the business architecture, typically referred to as business intelligence and/or customer relationship. In the application architecture, this must be addressed by business intelligence and customer relationship systems. Likely, there's a strong dependency between these applications. This dependency is also defined in the application architecture. The functional dependency between the processes business intelligence and customer relationship is laid out in the business architecture.

- **Data or information architecture**: Business processes rely on information. This is translated from data and the data flows between applications. Data flows and data processing that defines the requirements for data input and desired output to steer the enterprise are part of the data and information architecture. The data architecture defines the data models, including how data is stored and securely transported between systems.

  During the course of this book, I will discuss the data-driven enterprise and how this is addressed in modern EA. Data-driven architecture has become crucial for almost any enterprise. Every decision that an enterprise takes must be based on data. Data is constantly gathered and analyzed, providing continuous feedback to the enterprises on how products and services are performing in the markets. We will see that EA is already addressing this: in The Open Group Architecture Framework (TOGAF), data is the most important asset in architecture, driving the business.

- **Technological architecture (IT)**: This architecture defines the infrastructure that hosts the applications and the data. It comprises all technical elements such as network connectivity, compute, storage, and interfaces.

These are not independent components; in EA they are heavily correlated. This also implies that we need governance to control the components and make sure that they form a coherent overarching model that drives the business and supports the enterprise's strategy. EA is therefore also about planning. If we define a strategy, then we also create a plan to reach the goals that are set in the strategy. You can set a destination, but without knowing how to reach the destination, you will never reach it. You need to know the route, the ways of transportation, possible roadblocks that you might encounter, and how to get around these roadblocks. You would probably also want to know how long the journey will take you and what the costs are of that journey unless you have unlimited resources. It's no different with EA and the subsequent enterprise strategic planning. Plan and planning can't be separated.

A plan requires planning and decision-making for various disciplines in the enterprise. It includes details on

- Investments

- Workforce

- Operations

- Security and risk management

- Program management

- Skills management

- Change management

Decisions need to be taken on every aspect:

- Do we have the right resources with right skills?

- Do we have budgets?

- Do we have budgets allocated?

- Can we run this program on time and budget?

- Do we know what risks we are facing?

- What will be the costs if we delay?

- What are mitigating actions and fallback scenarios?

- What costs are involved with that?

- Is the organization ready for change?

All of this must be considered in drafting the enterprise architecture – on strategic, business, and eventually the technical level. But where do we start? The answer: by getting some help from architectural frameworks that guide us in setting up the enterprise architecture. We will learn in the next sections, but first we will discover where EA sits in the organization.

Understanding the Position of EA

From the previous section, we learned that EA is at the top of the architectural chain: it drives all other architectures in the enterprise. Better said, EA provides guardrails and policies for doing architecture on various levels, both business and technological oriented. It's shown in Figure 1-3.

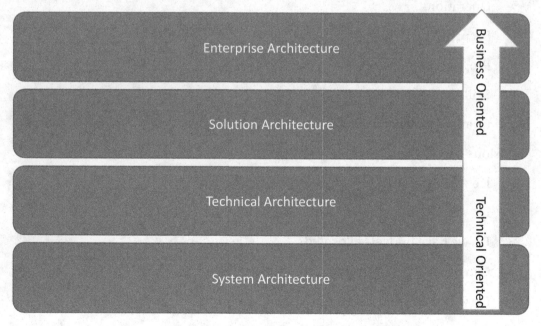

Figure 1-3. *Position of enterprise architecture in other architectures*

Note that we now have different, even overlapping definitions of the various layers of architecture than we have discussed in the previous section.

- **System architecture**: This architecture lays out how systems are built and configured. The architecture is low level detailed on the use of software and hardware components, describing exactly what type of hardware is used and what software, including operating systems and middleware. Just mentioning that a system runs Linux is not sufficient in this architecture; it must mention the used Linux version and how the operating system is configured, for instance, what security policies have been applied. This is analogue to the technological architecture that we defined as one of the EA components. To avoid misunderstanding, we often refer to this as the IT or infrastructure architecture.

- **Technical architecture**: This architecture contains the details on the technical landscape and shows how systems are related to each other. It shows the data flows, applications, and services used to fulfill solution requirements. As an example, the technical architecture shows how an application is connected to a specific database or how the application is communicating to the outside world, using Internet gateways or other connections. This is mapped to the data and application architecture. The details of the configuration of the database server are part of the system architecture. The technical architecture will show what instances the database holds (think of databases with customer data, where every region of the enterprise has its own database instance); the system architecture will tell that the server runs SQL on top of a Windows operating system and in what versions.

- **Solution architecture**: This architecture is about fulfilling specific business requirements and aims on creating value. It shows how the technical architecture and the systems are brought together to create a solution addressing a specific need of customers. So, we have a technical solution showing what databases the enterprise has and how they functionally look like, and we have a system architecture telling that the database is running Windows and SQL. But that's not a solution. A solution answers the question how systems and technical architectures help solve a business issue or problem. In this case, the business requirement might have been to provide a solution to store customer data per region in a database. That resulted in a solution choosing for a specific setup of the database and how this setup can be technically fulfilled. System and technical architecture must be aligned with the business architecture.

- **Enterprise architecture**: This is the overarching architecture that holds the business strategy, defines the governance on architecture on various levels, and drives the digital transformation of the entire enterprise. This architecture doesn't just cover the one solution for regional databases holding customer information, but for every system in the enterprise landscape. The enterprise architecture forms the guardrails for any other architecture in the enterprise, including a clear definition of processes to work with architecture.

We could say that the enterprise architecture sets the greater goal of the enterprise and eventually drills down to the specific system architectures of products and services that the enterprise delivers to its customers. It's crucial to understand that these different architecture layers can't exist independently from each other. The reason for this is that every layer in architecture starts with the customer requirements. In essence, architecture must structure the requirements and translate these into specifications for a product or a service. As we have seen, we need resources to do that. We need a planning to have the appropriate resources available in time. And the architect needs to understand how various technical components are linked together in fulfilling requirements.

There are methodologies that address all of this in a structured approach. Let's look at one of these methodologies. The Quality Function Deployment (QFD) and the House of Quality (HOQ) are examples. Both are included in the management strategy framework Six Sigma and "match" perfectly to the goal of EA.

QFD – originally a Japanese concept – is a process that drives planning for products and services, comprising four stages: product planning, product design, process planning, and process control. Japanese car builders Toyota and Mitsubishi apply QFD in their production process. The aim of QFD is customer satisfaction and that can already be achieved by small changes in the product. That's the reason to explore every aspect of the product individually. For example, the customer experience and satisfaction about a car can be improved by changing just one component, for instance, the seats. It's not about changing the entire architecture of the car, but only the seats. Nonetheless, the seats are an integrated part of the car.

- **Product planning**: Identify and prioritize customer requirements, using the Voice of the Customer (VOC).

- **Product design**: Ideas and concepts are developed, leading to product specifications.

- **Process planning**: Define how the product must be developed.

- **Process control**: The actual production is planned, including testing and validation against the specifications as set in the VOC. In this stage the HOQ is used for validation.

The whole cycle, however, starts with the Voice of the Customer (VOC), the customer requirements. It's shown in Figure 1-4.

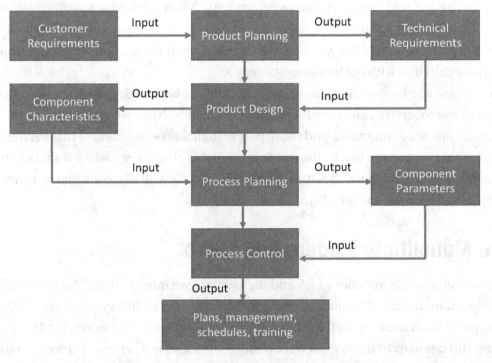

Figure 1-4. *The role of customer requirements in architecture using QFD*

This is part of the HOQ: with the VOC the relationship is defined between the customer requirements and the capabilities of the enterprise to design and deliver a product or service according to these requirements. This includes the determination of the market segments and the likeliness if the product will indeed "fit" the overall strategy of the enterprise. In the section about collecting business requirements, we will have a closer look at this methodology, since it's a very comprehensive way to translate requirements into products and services – and that's the core of EA.

Note that we will get into more detail on VOC in the section about gathering requirements.

We started this chapter with the fact that EA as a discipline is rather new. It originates in a time where system architecture was disconnected from the overall business strategy. To put it differently, systems couldn't adopt customer requirements fast. If the Voice of the Customer did reach the system engineers, then it took months and sometimes up to years to change the systems fulfilling these requirements. Complex, long-term programs were needed to have systems altered. In this modern age where customer requirements change rapidly and systems need to be adapted swiftly responding to these requirements, the "old" way of doing architecture isn't fit for purpose anymore. We need architecture that can address changes fast. We need this architecture on all levels – from the system architecture all the way up to EA. And we need EA to control changes and keep changes in line with the business strategy.

In the next section we will explore how architecture is changing from monolithic systems to microservices and how EA is impacted by this. Next, we will see that enterprises are becoming more and more part of digital ecosystems and that EA needs to address this ecosystem too. In the last section of this chapter, we will see that change management is crucial in architecture. As we go along, we will discover that any modern enterprise today needs modern EA.

From Monolith to Modern and Micro

Before we get into the trenches of EA and digitization, we must realize EA as a discipline was founded in the era of monolith system architecture. Monolith systems are designed as "one piece" and are very hard to change. New requirements that would lead to new features and changes to the system were tedious work and not seldom a risky operation.

The monolithic architecture of a system will limit the speed of change and the system itself will inevitably grow. In fact, it's almost inevitable that the system architecture will start to deviate from the original architecture making it even harder to innovate and address changing business needs while keeping the quality, availability, and reliability of the systems intact. This makes it mandatory to review and redesign the architecture of these monolithic systems; otherwise, they will slow down change or even cause business changes to come to a full stop.

Imagine what happens if the business strategy needs to be changed? We have seen examples of enterprises reconsidering their strategies due to changing market circumstances. It may lead to divestments or acquisitions. Either way, it will have huge impact on the subsequent architectures. Altering the system architecture might become a hazardous project. Examples are the carve-out of businesses in overarching enterprise resource planning (ERP) systems or the integration of systems.

Modern system architectures rely more and more on microservices. The concept is explained in Figure 1-5.

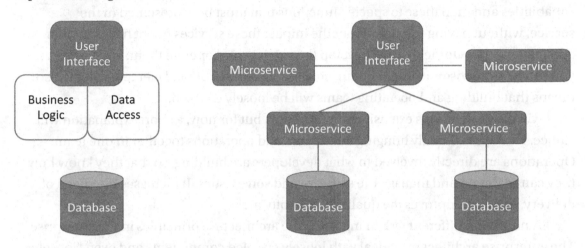

Figure 1-5. *Basic architectural views of monolithic vs. microservices*

So, a monolithic system or application holds all the functionality in one process and likely on one system, even on one or one group of servers. All the software components are contained in one library. In other words, all the work is done in one single process: storing data, processing data, up until presenting the data. It's all in one system. The monolithic system runs completely independent from other systems.

In microservices, each functionality is captured by a separate service. Presenting data or content is a separate service that can now connect to various platforms that hold data. If one platform is not responding, the presentation service can connect to another platform and make sure that the service to the customer is still delivered. Streaming services such as Netflix and Spotify make use of microservices. The presentation layer – viewing or listening to content – is a separate service. It can connect to various data systems holding that content, ensuring the most optimal, best performing route to the consumer.

Transforming to microservices has consequences for the enterprise architecture as well, as we will learn throughout this book. It comes with new rules for doing architecture as it aims for building systems as a set of services that are independently developed and deployed. Each microservice runs its own process and communicates through interfaces with other microservices. Each service fulfills a specific business capability with its own characteristics.

This has huge implications to the organization of architecture, development, and operating teams. In terms of architecture, business units can define their own capabilities and map these to specific functions that must be represented in the service, without having to worry about the impact these services might have on other applications. DevOps teams can develop the services and operate them: you build it, you run it. A microservice architecture consists of loosely coupled elements, but it also means that building and operating teams will be loosely coupled.

I will discuss DevOps extensively in this book, but for now, a short explanation will suffice. DevOps is literally bringing developers and operations together in one team. Operations are directly involved in what developers are building, so that they know how they can maintain and manage the software and solve issues. It increases the speed of delivery, but also improves the quality of the software.

EA now has a different task in maturing the architecture principles in the enterprise. The enterprise architect must deal with loosely coupled components and even "loosely coupled," better said, autonomously working teams who work on development and operations of these components. Without proper guardrails that have been derived from the overall enterprise business goals, this will become a risky undertaking. EA is the glue that binds it all together. From the EA it must be clear how the different services work together in providing the overall business services to customers of the enterprise. It also must provide clear formats on how teams should operate and collaborate in order to achieve the enterprise's business goals.

Loosely coupled components and different teams working on these components will create greater adaptability, but also more heterogeneity. The architecture will become more dynamic, with a much higher grade of granularity. Keeping the EA consistent with these dynamics is the new challenge for the enterprise architect.

In the next section, we will explore this changing role a bit more. This is just an introduction, however. In Chapter 6, we will discuss this in more detail.

The Role of EA in Microservices

What's the role of the enterprise architect when enterprises shift to microservices? Before we get into that, it's good to point out the benefits of microservices.

- **Agility**: Teams don't develop an entire application, but only a service that is part of the application, for example, the database service or the payment functionality in an app. This way a team only needs to worry about that specific service. This decreases the development time dramatically.

- **Resiliency**: The idea behind microservices is that it decreases the risks of a single point of failure. The rationale is that only parts of the application are updated, preventing a long downtime for the entire application. The same applies if a service is hit by an incident. The application will be impacted, but the affected service – and with that, the incident – can be isolated. This does imply that enterprises have proper end-to-end monitoring in place that allows for deep root cause analysis when incidents occur.

- **Scalability**: Microservices are developed in such way that they can be deployed in multiple applications and systems. That makes them scalable.

- **Business impact**: An important factor in the EA. Because of agility, resiliency and scalability development cycles are shorter and systems suffer less from downtimes. This immediately shows in the business results. Less downtime means lower costs, to start with. But also customers will be happier since services are less interrupted and products continuously improved. This will show in the total revenue of the enterprise. There's a risk to this as well: if development does slow down, there will be cost of delay since customer expectations will increase over time, and with slower development or service breaches, these expectations will not be met. It takes more time to regain trust than to build initial trust.

The enterprise architect obviously isn't expected to program microservices, but they will need to understand them. They need to understand how the system landscape is built and how it addresses the business requirements. The enterprise architect will have an overarching overview of the entire business and system landscape and that is crucial when the enterprise is shifting toward microservices. Typically, with the adoption of microservices, also DevOps as a development methodology will be adopted, creating teams that develop and operate the service. Without an enterprise view, loosely coupled will soon become "completely detached."

Besides, it's very unlikely that all systems will be transformed to microservices. Most enterprises – unless they are completely cloud-born – will have legacy systems that they need to operate for years to come. A lot of enterprises have started their journey into cloud and cloud native, but they are still earth-born migrants. We will talk extensively about this in Chapter 2.

The enterprise architect will guard the application portfolio. What systems and applications are linked to what business process? For example, if an application allows customers to place orders, then the system needs to have connections to an online store and a payment service as a minimum. Then we already have to major business processes that we must address: one is making sure that products are available in the store and, second, that customers can pay for these products in the store. But there's so much more that the architect must consider. What happens if the order is aborted during the ordering process, or a payment fails? How resilient is the process and how resilient are the systems?

What is the criticality of the process and, with that, of the system and the applications? Is there a business case to change the system to microservices, meaning how much effort will it take in terms of funding and resources? More important, what will be the profit for the business and the benefits for the customer? There might be short-term trade-offs and benefits for the longer term, for instance, in the workload for operations. If systems are designed in a leaner fashion using modern technologies, the enterprise might save costs in operations.

The enterprise architect will draw a plan that includes all these aspects and at the same time "guard" the impact on the remaining systems. This also means that they have to do a risk assessment, ensuring that the lights stay on during the transformation. New systems designed according to the microservices architected need to integrate with the legacy systems. Plus, there must be skilled resources available to do these integrations and operate the legacy systems.

It's good practice to work through this in phases:

1. **Assess**: Explore the benefits of building microservices and the business case.

2. **Plan:** In this stage the enterprise architect must validate the assessments and the business case against the overall architecture. This includes exploring the roadmap for transition and transformation from the current state – the present mode of operation – to the future state, or the future mode of operation.

3. **Execute:** The architect must choose the right technology stack and define guidelines for the DevOps teams using runbooks.

4. **Continuous feedback:** Iterations must be closely monitored; results are continuously looped back to improve the next iteration. Fail points and gaps must be identified in the earliest stage possible and mitigated. This phase is all about quality management.

These phases are never a one-time off, but a continuous loop. Enterprises are never done. Businesses will always change and thus business demands. Hence, a transformation is never done. You will indeed recognize the essence of DevOps in this, as shown in Figure 1-6.

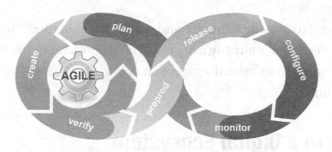

Figure 1-6. *The DevOps cycle*

DevOps is addressing the management of this process. Modern EA will therefore have to adopt DevOps. The activities in DevOps are guided by EA, especially in the plan phase where the enterprise architect defines:

- Business metrics (voice of the customer, customer satisfaction, just to name two)

- Production metrics (including business objectives and service-level agreements)

- Requirements definition

- New features and functions priorities and fixes

- Release plan (business case)

- Security aspects

This is next executed in create, verify, preprod, release, and configure. These activities are all build activities: creating the design, verifying the design against the requirements, building the first version and testing it, and configuring and releasing the build to production where it can be used.

In the monitoring phase, the EA again plays a critical role, since this is the phase where the metrics are actually measured:

- Performance and availability of the environment, including IT infrastructure and the application

- End-user response and experience

Although I talk about DevOps here, it should be DevSecOps in fact. Security is not something that we put on top of DevOps cycles but integrate with that cycle. This will be discussed later in this book.

In short, EA needs to provide structure and, with that, guidance. That's the role of the enterprise architect. That's already a big task, but it gets a bit more complex. The enterprise doesn't stand on its own: it's part of an ecosystem. We will learn more about that in the next section.

Including EA in a Digital Ecosystem

This book is about a transformation to modern enterprise architecture. A lot of enterprises are amid digital transformation where they find themselves digitally connected with other enterprises, suppliers, public authorities, financial institutions, and of course, their customers. Enterprises do not stand on themselves anymore, but they are continuously connected. Enterprises have become part of digital ecosystems. It implies that architecture should be focusing on the enterprise's position in a digital ecosystem.

What is a digital ecosystem? It's a network, first and foremost. It connects enterprises, but that's not all. In this network the connected enterprises interact with each other with the goal to create value in that network. To enable the interaction across the ecosystem, the enterprises need to have a shared mental model across the ecosystem and a digital platform that allows them to connect and interact.

A shared mental model enables shared understanding on how companies in an ecosystem should act in various situations. Since the value for all companies in the ecosystem is created through cooperation in that system, the sole interest of one enterprise is not leading, but the interests of the entire ecosystem. Decisions are jointly taken to achieve the maximum value for the customers that are also part of that ecosystem. An important principle in decision-making within an ecosystem is second-order thinking. It means that one enterprise in the system doesn't immediately try to solve an issue but analyzes the issue with other companies in the ecosystem. As an ecosystem, the consequences of decisions are thought through, and after assessment of these consequences, the best solution for the system is chosen.

To operate an ecosystem efficiently, we need a shared platform. In many modern enterprise architectures, a shared, foundational platform will probably be – or become – a key artifact. Amazon and Microsoft are great examples of such platforms that allow enterprises to share technology and business propositions. Amazon uses its own AWS to launch services and products, but also allows other companies to use the platform in many varieties. They can offer goods on the Amazon reseller platform or share content through AWS, like Netflix does. Companies can work together in the development of services and products, using the technologies of Microsoft or Google. Think, for instance, of research programs for new medicines, using the AI engines of the different platforms. Developers can collaboratively work on the same code using platforms such as GitHub and find solutions much faster than they could when they work within the silo of just one enterprise. The success of these shared platforms also defines the success of the users of the platforms: the ecosystem. However, it requires a different mindset. Participants in the ecosystem must be focused on the collective purpose and shared goals and have a joint mission to create value as a collective of companies.

The modern enterprise is a connected enterprise in a digital ecosystem. This has introduced complexity over the years. The ecosystem of the enterprise has grown and will grow dramatically, as the number of stakeholders in that ecosystem has grown and will grow with it. It creates tremendous possibilities for communication, interaction, and growing business opportunities, but it also causes complexity and potential risks. The ecosystem is as strong as the weakest partner in the system. That needs to be controlled to protect the enterprise. The enterprise architecture must address this by acknowledging that the enterprise is relying on partners and its stakeholders in the ecosystem.

This shift in architecture is often referred to as emergent architecture – architecture that develops "as it goes along," agile responding to changes and addressing opportunities without the constraints of a standing architecture. Enterprises in digital ecosystems need to adapt and adopt fast. Changing the architecture takes time and especially software developers felt they were slowed down by the architectural process. Why would you architect systems in the first place? The answer to that question is that an enterprise needs consistency. But are there other ways to stay consistent, yet embed agility in the architecture? That's where the idea of the North Star came in: an orientation point, rather than something that's already completely fixed. The North Star guides, gives direction, but doesn't tell exactly how to reach the destination.

The North Star will provide insights on where the enterprise is and where it's heading for, ideally as part of the ecosystem. The "architecture" as such will be very lightweight, pointing out key systems and interaction touchpoints with other systems inside and outside the enterprise. The North Star will point out business critical processes and what the dependencies are within the ecosystem and show the patterns that are used in architecture, aiming for value creation as collaborative output of the ecosystem.

It should be simple. It should be accessible to every stakeholder in the ecosystem. It should be easy to update and address changes very swiftly. However, the North Star should not have to change very often. If that's the case, it probably holds too much low-level details. The details should be captured in underlying, forthcoming system and technical architectures. Changes in the North Star will most certainly lead to changes in the more detail architectures and that's why change management on every level in EA is crucial. In the final section of this chapter, we will discuss this.

Short and simple, a North Star is less strict than architecture. However, enterprises still need EA to control architectures and that includes these North Stars. Without the overarching governance of EA, the enterprise faces the risk of drifting away from the enterprise's mission. Yet, modern EA must adopt emergent architecture and North Stars, without a doubt. We will learn about that when we discuss the EA frameworks of Zachman and TOGAF in this chapter. The reason is clear: the existing frameworks are indeed too rigid and need to be adapted to the challenges of the modern enterprises. But it's too bold a statement to say that enterprises don't need EA any longer. We will discuss this in the next section when we explore the benefits of EA.

The Benefits of Enterprise Architecture

This could be a very short section by stating that the biggest benefit of EA is having control. Obviously, the list of benefits is a bit longer, varying from rather soft, immeasurable benefits to hard, measurable, and proven benefits. An important study on the benefits is done by Eetu Niemy of the University of Jyväskylä in Finland. (*Enterprise*

Architecture Benefits: Perceptions from Literature and Practice, 2006: `https://jyx.jyu.`
`fi/bitstream/handle/123456789/41370/Article_EA_Benefits.pdf?sequence=1&`
`isAllowed=y`). Remarkably, the improved alignment between IT and the business
was identified as one of the major benefits. The problem, however, is how do we
measure that?

In the previous section, we acknowledged that EA is aiming to provide consistency.
From EA we set some ground rules in how we manage the enterprise, what markets the
enterprise targets, and with what products and services. That's captured in the mission
of the enterprise. Next, we need a strategy to get products and services to the identified
markets and customers. Enterprises need technology to develop and deliver products
and services.

From the EA we aim for a common, holistic business vision: every part of the
enterprise focuses on the same mission and makes sure the strategy is followed
through. If we allow departments or even individuals to deviate and take other turns,
the enterprise will drift away from fulfilling the mission. This implies that all parts of the
enterprise collaborate.

Collaboration between business units is served with standardization. That's not
a benefit on itself from EA, but standardization will lead to economies of scale and
reduced costs. That's something that we can measure. In fact, in the study by Niemy,
reduced costs are the most mentioned benefits from EA, directly followed by improved
alignment between businesses.

One more benefit of EA that was mentioned was improved change management.
The debate is whether change management is really a benefit of EA or a requirement
for working with EA. We will see that change management is an important step in
creating architectures using the various EA frameworks. Architecture without change
management processes in place will lead to uncontrolled and undocumented changes
to the architecture and, as a result, to unpredicted outcomes for the business. In the final
section of this introduction chapter, we will discuss the need of change management in a
bit more detail.

Using Zachman and TOGAF

As an introduction, we've looked at components that form the enterprise architecture, what it takes to get governance in place, and what the benefits would be of EA. It would help to have frameworks that put components and governance comprehensively together to guide architects in working under and with EA. The good news is that these frameworks exist, but it takes some time to learn working with them.

The two best known and probably also most used EA frameworks are Zachman and The Open Group Architecture Framework (TOGAF). In this section we will explore these frameworks and learn how to start working with them. Now, this is not a book on these frameworks themselves, but a basic understanding of Zachman and TOGAF is required to see why we need to evaluate to modern EA – still using these frameworks.

The Framework of Zachman

John Zachman perceived architecture as a methodology to describe complex things in any format for different purposes. The model is defined by 36 categories that are used to describe these complex environments. That could be an airplane or, indeed, an enterprise. To describe the enterprise, Zachman recognizes six perspectives:

1. **Scope**: Objectives, size, shape, and relationships of the enterprise.

2. **Enterprise model**: Conceptual business models and business goals.

3. **System model**: Logical processes, data models, workflows, and functions of business components.

4. **Technology model**: Information systems.

5. **Engineering model or detailed representation**: Detailing the technology model with tools, programming languages, and any other supporting technology. This contains detailed requirements for all types of technology.

6. **Operational model or functioning enterprise**: Operational management of the enterprise.

On the horizontal axe, the viewpoints are plotted. The result is matrix that forms a blueprint for the enterprise. The original model is shown in Figure 1-7.

	What? DATA	How? FUNCTION	Where? NETWORK	Who? PEOPLE	When? TIME	Why? MOTIVATION
SCOPE {contextual} Planner	List of things important to the business	List of processes the business performs	Locations in which the business operates	List of organisations important to the business	List of events/cycles significant to the business	List of business goals / strategies
BUSINESS MODEL {conceptual} Owner	e.g., Semantic model	e.g., Business process model	e.g., Business logistics system	e.g., Work flow model	e.g., Master schedule	e.g., Business plan
SYSTEM MODEL {logical} Designer	e.g., Logical data model	e.g., Application architecture	e.g., Distributed system architecture	e.g., Human interface architecture	e.g., Processing structure	e.g., Business rule model
TECHNOLOGY MODEL {physical} Builder	e.g., Physical data model	e.g., System design	e.g., Technology architecture	e.g., Presentation architecture	e.g., Control structure	e.g., Rule design
DETAILED REPRESENTATIONS {out-of-context} Subcontractor	e.g., Data definition	e.g., Program	e.g., Network architecture	e.g., Security architecture	e.g., Timing definition	e.g., Rule specification

Figure 1-7. *The Zachman Framework*

The problem with the original model was that it's still hard to get to real architecture. It was more a declarative model than a "driving" model that guided in doing architecture. Yet, Zachman had a huge impact, being the first model that showed that information technology and system design were closely integrated with business processes, planning, and management. Zachman was also the first to identify different stakeholders and perspectives in architecture. That has been key in EA. Stakeholders have different perspectives on business goals and outcomes and therefore have different requirements to how goals and outcomes should be achieved.

Essential in the Zachman Framework is the reasoning: What is the reason for an enterprise as a whole or a stakeholder within the enterprise to conduct a certain activity and what are the dependencies with other stakeholders in the enterprise? By describing the enterprise in a six-by-six matrix, relationships between enterprise artifacts (vertical axe) and views (horizontal axe) are immediately clear. It's the strength of this model.

A Better Guidance with TOGAF

Zachman does provide insights in how the enterprise operates, but it doesn't guide in how to do architecture very well. It doesn't provide a step-by-step approach on how to put together an architecture. For that, TOGAF is a more comprehensive framework. The key element in TOGAF is the Architecture Development Method (ADM) cycle. It's a cycle, since TOGAF perceives architecture as a continuous activity.

The ADM cycle is shown in Figure 1-8.

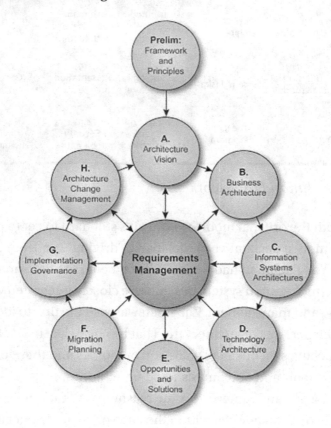

Figure 1-8. *The ADM cycle in TOGAF*

Like Zachman, TOGAF starts with the overall purpose and goals of the enterprise's business and then defines the logical models for information systems and lastly the technology to support these business models. It uses the classic BAIT model for this: business, application, information, and technology. TOGAF then reasons as follows:

- What business problem are we solving?

- What interface (application) do I need to get to the information that I need to solve the business problem?

- What information do I need to solve the business problem?

- What technology serves the access and analyses of the information best to solve the business problem in the most optimized way?

In this way of reasoning, we can already see that there are choices to be made. That's what architecture is about: providing options, analyzing options, and choosing the best option to solve the problem. TOGAF helps in making these choices, first by continuously referring to the requirements. It's the heart of ADM: What do I really need? Then TOGAF helps the architect in recognizing opportunities and making the right decisions in the solutions. In the next phase, we define how we can implement the solutions, or "how do we get from A to B"? That's a transition and it needs to be managed. The architecture of the solution must be governed to make sure that it keeps fitting the overall purpose and goals of the enterprise. In the extension of the ADM cycle, we can perfectly see how this architectural reasoning works in TOGAF, as shown in Figure 1-9. In this case we see how the technical solution is created.

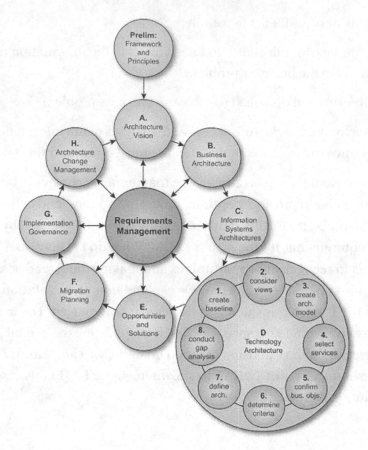

Figure 1-9. *Detailing of Phase D – technology architecture in TOGAF*

Creating the technology architecture now starts with setting the baseline, or where are we coming from? Next, we must consider the different views and corresponding options that we have to draft the solution. We select the appropriate building blocks and validate these against the business requirements. We must also perform a gap analysis: Is our solution really fitting the requirements and is it delivering the expected value? If not, we must go back to the stage where we are considering views and options. If the solution is a good match, then we can proceed to implementation.

Here's the big difference between Zachman and TOGAF. Zachman is advocating to have the enterprise laid out in every single detail. The model serves as a blueprint for the enterprise. His argument for this was that information systems serving the business should be treated as any complex system that we document at the lowest detail possible. Systems must be documented in great detail so that engineers know exactly what parts of a system need to be repaired or changed. This might be true for a lot of legacy, monolithic, and business critical systems, but in a world of fast-changing digital ecosystems, we will spend more time in documenting and maintaining the blueprints than we are spending on the actual changes that support the business.

Still, the EA must cover all aspects of the business, all architectural domains. As we've seen in the previous sections, we need guidance in how we can address business demands in our systems and applications. The reason for that is that there always constraints. We've listed these in the first section: funding and resources are limited. However, the same limits apply in setting out the EA. An overall EA that covers the entire enterprise will absorb a great amount of time and thus money and human resources – if we have resources with the appropriate skills. Again, covering the entire enterprise in an extensive EA might not be agile enough for the modern enterprise. We need a different approach. TOGAF provides that.

We must look at the different architecture domains: business, data, applications, and technology. Now we can follow two approaches.

1. **Vertical**: We can divide an enterprise into verticals, each representing a specific segment of the business. Sometimes these segments are referred to as business lines, units, or clusters. These different segments representing a business sector can have its own EA, capturing the EA BAIT-domains business, applications, information, and technology. The challenge here is the integration between the different segments to serve the entire enterprise and deliver value to the enterprise as a whole.

2. **Horizontal**: The BAIT domains are captured on the level of the entire enterprise. These will function as "super domains" covering every aspect of the enterprise throughout all the underlying businesses. The business lines, units, or clusters all follow this overall EA. Specifics are detailed in separate product and service architectures. There will be a need for these separate architectures and that's the major challenge in this approach – fitting the EA to the specific business needs of business sectors.

None of these two approaches will cover all aspects of the EA. But here's one of the most common pitfalls in EA: trying to capture every single detail of the enterprise in one go. There's no need to aim for a complete architecture from the beginning. EA is per default an iterative process. That's the reason why ADM is presented as a cycle. We as architects consider views, viewpoints, and options and translate these into artifacts that build the architecture, guiding the composition of solutions. That's not a one-off exercise. On the contrary, in modern EA we need to make this an agile process, wherein we can consider options to various views and viewpoints inside the enterprise and outside, in the ecosystem.

To avoid the pitfall of trying to be as detailed as possible and complete from the beginning, we should define a target architecture. Indeed, this can be a North Star. Next, we can use ADM to iterate toward the target architecture. And remember that this target architecture might change over time, so we need to consider an architectural methodology that is able to adopt these changes fast and that they can be included in the iteration cycles.

Sounds cool, but how would that work? Like any other agile project. We define the baseline, so we know where we are coming from. We can call this the "as-is" situation, IST, or present mode of operation. Next, we define the target based on the mission and goals of the enterprise. This is the to-be situation, or SOLL, or future mode of operation. We can do this for the enterprise as a whole, but we also need to derive target architectures for the various business sectors. We will call these architecture instances.

Every target architectural instance must contain the objectives and concerns of the various stakeholders. Lastly, we must ensure that all instances serve the overall enterprise's mission and goals. This must be part of the transition: every architectural instance must be validated against the overarching target architecture or North Star. Main question: Is it contributing to the overall value that the enterprise must bring to its customers?

Architectures are by default evolutionary in a modern enterprise. Business demands will require constant change to the architectures. However, since the overall target architecture or North Star merely captures the direction of the enterprise, these will not change frequently. They will allow for incrementally adopting changes in the underlying business, information, and technology architectures. In conclusion, the overall EA is likely more a directive, guiding target architecture, where details are incrementally captured in underlying architectures as long as the overall enterprise strategy is not put at risk and delivery of value in the enterprise's ecosystem is safeguarded. TOGAF is a great aid in defining architectures on different levels and guiding the iterative process of defining and working under architecture.

Target architectures and subsequently the target operating model are the main topics of Chapter 2.

Using IT4IT to Mature the Modern Architecture

There's at least one more framework that we should mention in this book and as an introduction to modern EA. We discussed Zachman as a methodology to create an enterprise blueprint and TOGAF as a method to create architectures. TOGAF is coming from the business perspective, but as we concluded earlier in this chapter, IT – or digital – has become more and more important to any business. Modern enterprises are digital enterprises. How do we match the IT architecture with the business architecture, also taking the digital transformation into account? IT4IT of The Open Group is a framework that's helping with that.

IT4IT works with value streams. The four streams are shown in Figure 1-10.

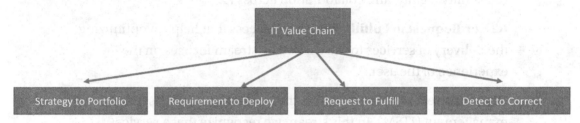

Figure 1-10. *The value streams in IT4IT*

In essence, IT4IT is what architecture is about: to deliver value. Enterprises develop and deliver products and services based on market and customer demand. Customers will only purchase that product or service when it delivers value to them. Hence, architecture is driven by value. IT4IT describes the full digital chain of development and delivery, from initiation to realization. IT4IT helps in organizing IT management and supporting the digital enterprise. More important, it enables IT to really add value to the business, since if focuses on the outcome for the customers, stakeholders, and end users of products and services.

The four value streams aim to create value through IT and IT service management. We could say that IT4IT integrates business, systems, and technology architecture by looking through the lens of the user of IT – and IT product needs to add value to the product or service that a customer purchases and uses. The product needs to fulfill the requirements but must also allow for detection of issues before the user experiences issues. Value is not just the delivery of the product but also the management of it, the quality of the service that comes with the product. A product that has all the desired features but breaks at first use has no value to the user. Next, a product that doesn't get regular updates and upgrades will decrease in value. So, we need architecture to address this lifecycle. IT4IT is a framework that can help with these challenges.

Let's briefly look at the four main value streams.

- **S2P or Strategy to Portfolio**: This is the value stream that manages the alignment between the business strategy and the IT portfolio that is required to fulfill the strategy.

- **R2D or Requirement to Deploy**: This stream helps to define the requirements to build and deploy IT services. The stream aims for high-quality, predictable results for the business while focusing on reusability, agility, and collaboration across IT.

- **R2F or Request to Fulfill**: This is the process that helps in optimizing the delivery of services to the users. The stream focuses on the experience of the user.

- **D2C or Detect to Correct**: This is the integration with IT service management (ITSM). In this stream we recognize that a service needs to be managed to maintain the value for the user. It uses the ITSM processes such as incident management, problem management, configuration management, and – very important – change management. D2C supports in service-level monitoring, detection, and remediation of issues so that the user is not (severely) impacted by issues.

So, now we have several frameworks that we can work with as an architect and set out the guidelines for our modern EA. The question we could ask ourselves is, do we really need all of this? It's a question that we can't simply answer with a yes or no. All of these frameworks have their benefits and can add to composing a viable EA. The IT4IT framework is a good starting point to describe the lifecycle of our digital products, assuming that our enterprise is amid digital transformation, the driver for modern EA. It helps in defining the flow of the product, aligning the portfolio with the business strategy, developing, releasing, and managing the product.

We can use TOGAF to describe the various architectural artifacts and the target architecture, coming from the present mode of operation (or IST or baseline) to the future mode of operation (or SOLL). ADM helps in defining the steps to get to the different architectures that we need to address the requirements and the overall enterprise strategy.

The different frameworks and models help in maturing the EA. However, there's one question that we didn't answer yet. Is this covering the needs of the modern, digitized enterprise that must respond to swiftly changing needs as a result of market trends and user demands? Are these models agile enough? The Open Group has released a new framework that seems to be more suitable to modern enterprises: Open Agile Architecture (O-AA). We will have a look at this in the next section.

Introduction to Floating Architecture with O-AA

Zachman and TOGAF have been around for several years. The issue with these frameworks is that they try to capture the entire enterprise in architecture. The risk of that is that these architectures tend to become blueprints, quite static, and hard to manage as enterprises get entangled in ecosystems with emergent architectures. We have drawn the conclusion that we need architectures that are able to adopt changes fast, addressing the constant change in market demands and customer requirements. However, we also need the enterprise to focus. They need a business strategy and, more so, a business focus. Within that focus, the business lines, units, or clusters need the freedom to operate fast. This challenge calls for a more or less "floating architecture": an architecture that stays above the water but is light and agile to adjust its course.

It almost seems a contradiction: the need for consistent architecture and at the same time the need for agility to operate the business. Open Agile Architecture (O-AA) might be an answer to this problem. O-AA addresses the challenges of the API-driven architecture. We have seen that enterprises have become of ecosystems, of (growing) networks of customers, partners, suppliers, and other stakeholders. An ecosystem is a connected world. Systems and stakeholders interact with each other. Modern architecture should tell you how components that are outside the enterprise must connect to systems inside the enterprise. If a component changes, there's no need to change the architecture of that component, since it's outside the enterprise, but it's required to validate and verify the touchpoint – this can, for instance, be an API – of that component to the systems inside the enterprise. These touchpoints are part of the technical architecture.

O-AA addresses this, first by identifying what a digital enterprise is. O-AA states that the digital enterprise is about *"applying digital technology to adapt or change"* the strategy of the enterprise, the product or service that the enterprise markets, and the experience that it delivers to customers and other stakeholders. O-AA also recognizes that the digital enterprise is changing its operating model to enable this transformation. Plus, *"the agile enterprise senses changes in its environment early and acts upon them decisively and rapidly."*

O-AA then describes the requirements to become an agile enterprise:

- Get rid of silos and aim for interdisciplinary collaboration, focused on the best outcome for the customer.

- To become agile, teams must be empowered to take decisions for themselves. Therefore, teams must be skilled to spot opportunities and quickly identify and classify risks.

There's a strong emphasis on collaboration, since O-AA sees that modern, agile enterprises are shackles in a connected chain. O-AA therefore focuses on the touchpoints that we discussed. These are crucial in defining the architecture. Figure 1-11 shows how O-AA sees touchpoints.

Figure 1-11. *Focus on customer centric in open agile architecture*

It immediately becomes clear that O-AA takes the perspective of the customer as the center of the architecture: the EA is completely customer-centric. Enterprises such as Amazon have adopted this view and even made it stronger. The key factor in the architecture of Amazon is the leading principle of "customer obsessed": the Voice of the Customer is setting the standards for the enterprise. The target operating model of the modern enterprise is about orchestrating these touchpoints, since O-AA predicts that touchpoints will multiply over time. Note that value stream mapping is part of O-AA, since any architecture – including an agile one – is about creating value.

With O-AA we conclude the introduction of EA and EA supporting frameworks. Let's put this to work, starting with collecting the business requirements. Before we do that, we must define our architecture vision: What do we want to achieve with architecture? That's the topic for the next section.

Starting with Architecture Vision

In the previous sections, we concluded that EA is about providing guardrails and guidance, coming from the overall business strategy, and supporting in putting together architectures that address the business needs. That strategy must be translated into an architecture vision.

The architecture vision is a term that is derived from TOGAF and forms the first phase in drafting the EA. If we translate this into simpler wording, then we could say that the vision comprises the guardrails for working under architecture in the enterprise. The vision contains the architecture statement (why do we need the EA) and next the directions for the business, information systems, and technology architecture. For all the good reasons, The Open Group themselves call the architecture vision the architect's elevator pitch. In the vision the architect explains the purpose of having an architecture.

It's tempting to leave the process of drafting the vision and just jump straight into the next phase, defining the business architecture. The reason for that is that very often the mission statement of the enterprise, the strategy, and goals are already documented somewhere else. Mission, strategy, and goals are however key in the vision. There's obviously no need to redo that work, but it's essential to assess and validate these artifacts as starting points for the business architecture. The architect needs to understand where the enterprise is coming from and what the goals are that it wants to achieve. Only then we can define the necessary steps that we must take to reach that goal.

Here's an interesting observation in modern enterprises. We have already noticed that goals might not be as fixed as in the earlier days. Markets change and customers change with them, quite rapidly. Still, the enterprise can set a mission and a strategy.

For example, the mission of a streaming service might be to become the world's leading service in streaming fantasy movies. The strategy might include the acquisition of a leading content studio. Now, what happens if the public suddenly turns its back to this type of content? We assume that the company has done some proper marketing research, proving that there's a market out there for this type of content. However, the market might change. Better said, the taste of the customer might change. Then it's interesting to know why that happens. There might be a new service offering revolutionary new content that's growing really fast.

This is the challenge in modern enterprises. Changes are inevitable, but they will occur at different speeds, impacting the strategy and the steps that an enterprise has defined to fulfill this strategy.

This is recognized in a model that is called ecocycles. These are used to distinguish, plan, and prioritize actions while involving every stakeholder in the activities that we need to deploy to take the step, taking changing circumstances like changing business environments into consideration. The principle of ecocycles is frequently used in agile/scrum. They provide a good guidance in helping a team to move forward.

The cycle itself looks very much like the DevOps cycle, and frankly, both are about develop, deploy, feedback, and renew. The ecocycle does that through the following:

- Accelerate growth during the birth phase

- Prolong life or increase efficiency in the maturity phase

- Eliminate unproductiveness during the creative destruction phase

- Leverage innovation in the renewal phase by connecting people in the teams

It's shown in Figure 1-12.

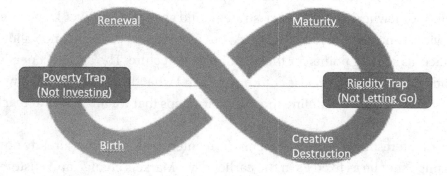

Figure 1-12. *The planning of ecocycles*

The poverty trap is the situation where ideas are born, but there's no focus or leadership to create real solutions from these ideas. We're not investing in solutions in the poverty trap. Rigidity is the opposite of that: sticking to ideas and habits that no longer add any value to the goals we want to achieve as a business. It's a cycle, so organizations – enterprises – will constantly be "on the move," going from new ideas to "destruction" of ideas that don't add to the business objectives and goals.

This is the reason why the vision needs to be part of the architecture lifecycle. Mission, strategy, and goals do not stand on themselves. They are part of cycles, and yet an integrated part of the architecture. Can we address this in drafting the architecture vision? Yes, by following these steps:

1. Recognize the change drivers

    a. Business goals

    b. Business principles

    c. Architecture principles

2. Identify objectives

3. Identify stakeholders and evaluate their concerns

4. Evaluate constraints

All of this requires input. We can't simply start on a blank piece of paper and start putting together our architecture. We need to collect the requirements. This is the topic for the next section.

Collecting Business Requirements

In the previous section, we learned that EA recognizes different stakeholders and perspectives. That makes collecting business requirements one of the most critical phases in EA. In this section we will learn how to get this done in the right way, using best practices.

The first step is to set the right goals and objectives. Indeed, this is done in the architecture vision. That vision should provide the guardrails to set the goals and objectives for projects. To get to the right goals and objectives, we must collect requirements. Requirements are not just a wishlist with must-haves, should-haves, and nice-to-haves. This is presumably the top mistake in requirements management.

The risk that we face is that requirements change very easily over time: gathering requirements is by default a dynamic process. The architect might find that he's working with requirements that in the minds of stakeholders have already changed. Or requirements might have changed due to changed market conditions or legislation. Nice-to-haves might have transitioned into must-haves or vice versa. The business case can be heavily impacted if requirements change or new requirements are identified, perhaps due to unforeseen circumstances (remember our ecocycles here).

TOGAF describes requirements as business scenarios. The purpose of a business scenario is to define what the outcome should be of a business process or an application. In the execution of that process or the application, the different actors are identified: Who is involved in the execution of the scenario? These actors are part of the business environment and make use of technology. All these artifacts influence one another and the outcome of the process or application.

In general, gathering requirements comes down to first set clear goals and objectives: What do we want to achieve? Then we must be sure who to talk to, the different actors such as stakeholders and users. But most important, architects should never make assumptions on requirements. Be specific and confirm every requirement: validate it with the relevant actors.

But this would be too easy in terms of gathering requirements. First of all, the architect is sure to miss some requirements. In modern EA, it's virtually impossible to capture everything. And there's no need to. If we define a modern enterprise as customer-centric, then we must focus on what value requirements bring to the customer. After all, that drives the business. Examples of value drivers can be the following:

- **Economic**: Lowering costs or increasing revenue.

- **Sustainable**: Lowering the CO_2 footprint, recycling of materials.

- **Ease of use**: Customers value a product or service when it's easy to use.

Of course, combinations of these drivers are possible and probably very desirable. The interaction with the customer has a major impact on setting the value drivers. Enterprises must adapt to this shifting interaction patterns. In the past, enterprises were organization-centric: the organization defined the product or service and the way how it was delivered to the customer. The only thing the customer was supposed to do was order or purchase the product; there was no or very limited influence of the customer in the way the product was designed or delivered.

That has changed dramatically. Most enterprises have become or are amid the transformation to a customer-centric organization. The customer has a big influence on the design, the production, and delivery of the product. Customer experience is captured in customer satisfaction scores, gathered through surveys and continuous feedback by means of ratings on the Internet.

The next level is the embedded customer, where the customer is part of the enterprise. Divisions, units, and teams of the enterprise interact directly with the customer to improve products and services or even parts of products of services. This demands a completely different setup of the enterprise. Teams not only interact directly with the customer, but they are self-organizing and mandated to take decisions. In extreme, the teams get a customer-paid salary. The enterprise now becomes a network organization, formed by micro-enterprises. Does this model work? The Chinese appliance manufacturer Haier has proven this with the Rendanheyi model, where teams are fully empowered to run their own business.

The difference in the three enterprise models is shown in Figure 1-13, where the last model is organized around micro-enterprises.

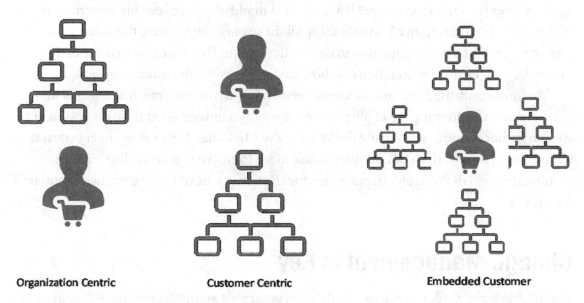

Organization Centric   Customer Centric   Embedded Customer

Figure 1-13. *The change in customer interaction*

The customer-centric and the embedded customer models clearly have advantages in collecting business requirements. These must come from the customers: The Voice of the Customer must be leading. Without customers, no enterprise will survive. The requirements must be proactively collected. The biggest pitfall is that architects assume the voice of the customer. A second pitfall is assuming that once we have collected requirements, these won't change. Customer experience changes and so do requirements. Collecting requirements must be done continuously and actively. What do customers seek in a product or a service? For example:

- Quality

- Service

- Delivery

- Choices

- Sustainable

- Safe

- Price

But this is not enough. We have to make this SMART: quantifiable and measurable. How fast does the customer want the delivery to happen? What is high quality? What options does the customer desire? If a product is made of 50% renewable materials, is that good enough to claim it's sustainable? All these parameters drive the value for the customer and thus the architecture to deliver that value. The price is actually mostly defined by the costs of production and how customers value the product or service.

We have confirmed that any business needs EA. We studied some frameworks that can help us in addressing the challenges of the modern enterprise and we discussed how we can gather requirements using the Voice of the Customer. We're all set to get started with drafting our modern EA. But there's one more thing we must establish since our architecture will definitively change over time. Hence, we need change management. In fact, it's key.

Change Management Is Key

Monolithic legacy, microservices, North Stars, emergent architectures, and ecosystems. The message is clear: modern enterprises are dealing with increasing complexity. They need to be agile and volatile, ready for constant change. Hence, good change management is essential.

Many companies have adopted DevOps as a new way of working. The golden rule in DevOps is "you build it, you run it," shifting responsibilities to business units and teams within these units. These teams become end-to-end responsible for the development and operations of products and services. You build it, you run it also means "you break it, you fix it." It's a major misperception that this is about technology and tools. Of course, automation plays a significant role in DevOps, but it's mostly about mindset and skills in the teams. What happens a lot though is that teams are really left on their own and get to decide everything – from the tools they use in their continuous integration/continuous deployment (CI/CD) pipelines up until the way of working. That can become a risk for the enterprise.

DevOps doesn't mean that an enterprise doesn't need EA and it certainly doesn't mean that it doesn't need change management. Change management is something different than feature management. DevOps teams will be responsible for the new releases of products and services with new features. But where do these new features come from? The answer is from requirements.

Since we've learned that requirements come from different stakeholders and will have various viewpoints that we must consider, the architect should validate the impact of requirements in terms of the overall business strategy. To put it differently, is a new feature adding value? What is the impact of developing new features? What resources are required, what are the costs, and what is the value driver? Product development and releases need to be controlled from architecture, aligning it with business objectives. It will raise the awareness in teams that every choice that they make in development and release comes with a consequence. And the enterprise should be better prepared to know what these consequences are.

We need change control. We must take the following aspects into account:

- Scope

- Time

- Resources

- Risks

- Stakeholder views

- Costs

- Quality

In change management the architect will be confronted with challenges. The different stakeholder views will likely be of great influence. The architect will have to assess these views and prioritize them, valuing the impact on the overall EA. But there's one challenge that is typically underestimated: resistance. Stakeholders will be affected by changes. Executives will, for instance, be asked to invest to finance the development of new features. Employees will have to change the way of working or confronted with extra work.

And don't forget the customer: If the Voice of the Customer is not captured well, enterprises might encounter resistance in the acceptance and adoption of new releases. Resistance is common and something enterprises must deal with. EA might not be able to solve this, but it can guide and direct in assessing the impact of a proposed change.

With that, we conclude this first chapter and hopefully it has become clear that any enterprise needs EA. However, enterprises have changed and will change in the future. They will become more part of ecosystems and they might transform into network organizations themselves, constantly dealing with changing business demands. EA has to evolve with these developments. In the next chapter, we will describe how EA can help in the transformation of enterprises.

Summary

If there's one thing you should remember after reading this chapter, it's that enterprise architecture (EA) is not solely about technology. It's about the business. In this chapter we explained that all enterprises need EA as a holistic, overarching model that drives the entire enterprise. We discussed the common EA frameworks such as TOGAF and Zachman and we noticed that these frameworks may not always serve the digital enterprise. In our digital age, enterprises are forced with constant changes, deriving from changing markets and customer demands. Enterprises are adopting new forms of architectures such as microservices and they adopt agile ways of working, all to keep up with the changes.

We've studied some other methodologies to capture these changes, mainly by putting the customer in charge of our enterprise. Capturing the Voice of the Customer has become essential. However, we must find ways to control the dynamics of these changes and that's where EA still serves us well: in keeping the enterprise architecture and the underlying architectures – business, information, and technological – consistent.

The big challenge is, how do we transform the enterprise to a digital enterprise and how does EA evolve with that? That's the topic of the next chapter.

CHAPTER 2

Transforming to Modern Enterprise Architecture

In the first chapter, we concluded that every enterprise needs enterprise architecture (EA). Every company needs a structure to function as a company and to deliver products and services to its customers. These structures change because the customers and their behavior change. The traditional models for EA will not cater for these changes. In this chapter we will explore how EA can help to transform the business to a modern enterprise. In fact, this chapter will be about business transformation and that's the domain of the enterprise architect. Next, new business models must be connected to systems of delivery. We will discuss new forms of enterprises, making them more agile, and enable them to transform from seller-driven to customer-driven.

Modern Enterprise Architecture

The big question to start with is probably, what is modern enterprise architecture? Over the years, frameworks such as TOGAF have been adapted and new frameworks have been introduced. We will look at the new edition of TOGAF (version 10) and O-AA in this section, but we must realize one thing in studying these frameworks, modern EA is about digital business. Are these new editions of the frameworks addressing the business aspects enough or are they mainly focused on technology?

Modern EA has to address modern objectives and challenges in enterprises. The biggest challenge isn't technology though, but the organization of the enterprise. A traditionally organized enterprise will not survive in the digital world. We need different organizations that are as flexible and agile as the products they release. We need organizations that embrace distributed ownership, meaning that teams that are responsible for the development of products or services take ownership of the entire lifecycle of that product or service.

39

© Jeroen Mulder 2023
J. Mulder, *Modern Enterprise Architecture*, https://doi.org/10.1007/978-1-4842-9066-8_2

Only distributed ownership can adopt new tech fast and respond to rapidly changing demands. There's no way that a traditional organization can do that. Development of new technology happens too fast, and customer demands change too fast to address this from a centralized, hierarchic organized body. That doesn't mean that we no longer need a centralized management of the enterprise. We do, but the role of that management changes. The governance of the modern enterprise changes drastically. Top management facilitates in modern enterprises. They provide guardrails and execute the business by advocating shift-left, moving responsibilities to small teams that are extremely close to the customers. For clarification, shift-left in the first place is about shifting testing closer to the first stages in the development process to help teams anticipating to issues in a very early stage. The idea is that the quality of development and the eventual product will improve if issues are detected as early as possible. This concept is leveraged to "shift-left thinking," including the idea of bringing development teams as close to the customer as possible with the same intent: to improve quality by capturing the demands of the customer in an early stage of development. We will discuss this further, including the shift-left movement and how we can embrace this in EA.

In the previous chapter, we talked about the way the customer changes the business. A model to address the rapidly changing demands of that customer is to embed the customer. The issue is that the customer as a singular entity doesn't exist anymore. Customers come in a lot of varieties and that has implications. A product needs to be as flexible and adaptable as the customer who buys the product.

Customers want customization, tweak, and tune a product or a service exactly to their liking. Next, they purchase the product in a lot of different ways. Some may still visit a physical store, but a growing number will buy products online. And even that's an oversimplification of the reality. They might buy it through a web store that's owned by the manufacturer, or through a platform or an app. Enterprises must facilitate the delivery processes for all these channels, including ordering, payments, packaging, shipping, and handling returns and complaints.

Customers share their experiences, also using different channels. They share these experiences in networks. An enterprise that wants to be successful must reflect these networks and need to be part of it to hear the Voice of the Customer. It has a huge impact on how the modern, digitalized enterprise operates. It has to mirror their communities in which their customers are. Since there will probably a lot of these communities, enterprises must reorganize themselves. That's where micro-enterprises are about: communities built around a service that is delivered by the enterprise. These communities must be built on an agile operating model.

To recap all of the previous discussions, modern enterprises require different thinking principles and thus a new form of EA. Let's dive into these thinking principles.

Adopting New Thinking Principles

Customers set the rules. They decide what they want, how they want it, when and where. They share experiences within communities and from there set new rules. Using modern methodologies of communication, experiences are shared at an incredible pace and this can have huge impact on enterprises within literally a matter of seconds.

There will be enterprises that will argue that they deliver commodity goods. What they're saying with that is that they need not listen to the customer. The product doesn't change: it's a commodity. Let's use an example. A tire is a commodity. It's made of rubber and it's round. Not much to design about that. If that was true, why are there so many different tires? The compound might vary, changing the character of the tire. The profile of a certain type of tire can be different than of other types, depending on the usage of the tire. And for what vehicle is it designed? Even the colors might vary.

Tire manufactories have figured out a long time ago that they too have to listen to the voice of the customer. Groups of customers demand different tires, specifying the exact needs to the products. Customers share experiences on platforms. Products are reviewed and scored, looping results back to the design process. If these results are not reflected in the development, customers will eventually turn their back on that product. It may be a very bold statement, but commodity doesn't exist anymore.

The most important lesson for the enterprise is that they need to empathize with their customers. Only when enterprises really empathize with their customers, they can deliver the outcome that the customer is looking for. Delivering that outcome and with that adding value to the customer will result in business success. Business success is something that we can measure in terms of revenue and profit, but the success itself is directly connected to the values and the experiences of the customer. We must find ways to embed this principle in our EA.

To put in other words, the delivery of desired customer outcomes and experiences is synonymous with the success of the enterprise. The challenge is the speed wherein the requirements of the customers change. They expect the enterprise to evolve their offerings at the same speed, continuously delivering products and services that provide that outcome. Hence, everything an enterprise does must be completely centered around the customer, the user of the products and services. The customer must be embedded.

We can try to define a new set of parameters to capture this embedding process.

- **Products**: The success of products is defined by a number of artifacts. These artifacts at their turn are defined by customer demands, needs, and requirements. That is set by the desired outcome for the customer or the user. We will look more closely at the Voice of the Customer, but already at this stage, it's important to appreciate that the outcome is the key driver for the success of a product or a service. It needs to add something to an experience that the customer has; it needs to represent value.

- **Perspectives**: How does the customer perceive the enterprise? That defines the perception of the product. For example, the product might be presented as "green" and with that environmentally friendly, but if the enterprise is not perceived to be green, then the product will not be accepted as green as well. On the contrary, the product might be perceived as sheer vanity, just "pretending" to be green. It might work against the enterprise as a whole.

- **Patterns**: This addresses behavior of customers. Behavior is influenced by perspectives. If the perspective is that our environment is damaged by products, the behavior will change in the requirement for more environmentally friendly products. That will evolve in a pattern: seeking for these products in more and different domains and eventually even "banning" companies that are not perceived as being environmentally friendly enough.

- **Platforms**: Customers are sharing experiences on platforms, but also use these platforms to generate new ideas. Enterprises might become an active actor on these platforms, but again, only if they have gained enough credibility to do so (perspectives). Enterprises must adopt this as a strategy to become a viable, trustworthy actor on these platforms to get and stay in direct contact with customers. Companies that are outside of these platforms and without any intention to become part of communities on the platforms are probably very short-lived in this modern age.

- **Promoter score:** The biggest driver of all for success. Is the customer
  a fan? If not, how do make him a fan? All of the previous Ps play a role
  in this.

We touched upon platforms and communities. Next, we must align the activities
of the community with the customer experience. This is the next step in defining our
modern EA. Reminder: Experience is key.

We can define the modern enterprise in three enterprise layers. They are shown in
Figure 2-1.

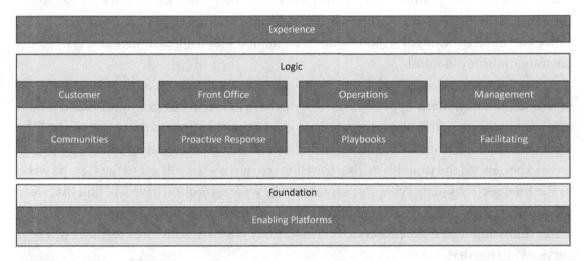

Figure 2-1. *The enterprise layers*

The logic contains the services and the corresponding workflows, ideally automated.
The foundation is the enabling platform.

The enterprise, however, is not a singular entity. It doesn't stand on itself, but it's part
of an ecosystem. EA should therefore address the way how to connect ecosystems. We
will learn how the enterprise architect can do this in the upcoming sections. We already
learned that enterprises need to empathize with the customer. Architects must focus
on embedding the customer by taking the journey of the customer as starting point.
Experience is key. That notice drives the entire architecture: by constantly viewing and
reviewing from the experience perspective.

We can use travel as an example, as we will do extensively in one of the next sections.
The traveler books a ticket at a travel agency, including a flight with an airline. At the
airport the traveler needs to go through customs, check in his luggage, and check in for
transfers. These services might be delivered by different companies that take care of

a specific service. It's the entire experience that counts: from the moment the traveler leaves home until he or she reaches the final destination.

All can be fine. The flight might be superb, customs very friendly, and the transfers right on time. One lost suitcase will ruin the complete travel – that one incident will define the whole experience. It will be worse when the traveler needs to find out who to attend to in order to retrieve the suitcase, realizing that it's not the travel agency or the airline that can help him because processes and systems are not connected.

To deliver a seamless experience, all systems in the ecosystem must connect to each other. Not only connect, but actually work with each other, event-driven, following the steps of the customer and triggering the right action at the right time and place. Processes need to be aligned; staff needs to be trained – all with customer and the customer journey in mind.

Just digitization doesn't solve this. Sure, enterprises can launch apps to help the customer. But how many apps does the traveler have to use in our example? Could it be one app connecting different microservices, even if they are from various companies? Start with thinking from the customer experience. If we do that as an architect and we have experienced the troubles during traveling ourselves – we will get to the Gemba walk in the final sections of this chapter: experience by walking around – we will find that we are not served by a zillion different apps, but by just one that is fully integrated. Under water there might be different services, dynamically scaled around the customer when services are needed.

Customer experience is leading in defining a modern EA. We need an organization that is able to capture these experiences proactively by connecting to customers using platforms. Management must facilitate the enterprise to operate in communities. The challenge is that enterprises don't stand on their own but are part of ecosystems. Customers move seamlessly through these ecosystems. It means that value streams – products and services that add value to a customer journey – are defined in that ecosystem. It's presented in Figure 2-2.

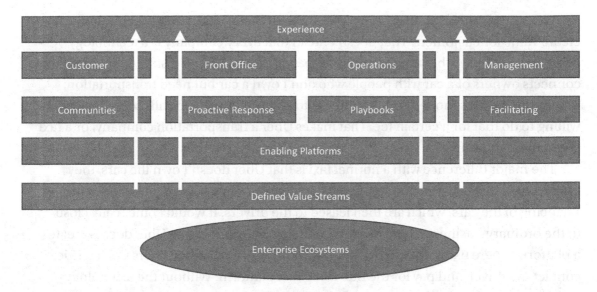

Figure 2-2. *The enterprise layers supporting the value streams as part of ecosystems*

In the next sections, we will explain how we transform the enterprise to a modern customer-driven enterprise – agile and capable of capturing and responding to customer journeys, addressing the five parameters that we previously discussed.

By now, it should be clear that EA encompasses more than just the IT of the enterprise, even in a digital transformation. Modern enterprise architecture focuses beyond managing IT assets. It aligns IT with the business. Through continuous review of products and services – from customer service and supply chain to operations and human resources – IT can optimize delivery and help the organization meet its strategic goals.

But the most important thing is that EA must focus on creating value. IT4IT can help in achieving this. We'll learn more in the next section.

Learning from IT4IT

In the first chapter we introduced several frameworks, among them IT4IT. IT4IT combines two essential chains: the value chain and the technology chain. Modern enterprises embed the customer and focus on value. To deliver that value, they need technology. Value and technology need to be connected in a logical way in the enterprise layers that we defined in the previous section: experience, logic, and foundation.

We can use the value streams of IT4IT for that. Better said, we use technology to create value for customers. That doesn't mean that every company is a technology company. Let's use Uber as example. In its bare essence, Uber is a sharing platform that connects owners of a car with people who don't own a car but need transportation. That's the business model. Someone needs to go from A to B and calls someone who is willing to do that for a certain fee. That makes Uber a transportation company, or a taxi company if you will.

The major difference with a normal taxi is that Uber doesn't own the cars, they are privately owned. (Fair enough, you could define a value stream that defines the financing of the cars, which are then leased to the drivers. It would come really close to the ordinary business model of a taxi company.) The only thing Uber does is create a platform where users and car owners can connect to each other. Users order a ride, contact the driver, and pay for the ride using that platform. Without the technology of that platform, Uber is quite useless. However, it still doesn't make Uber a technology company. They use technology to create value: an easily accessible way to order transportation.

Let's split this business model into different models that eventually create that value. We need these models to define the architecture. These models will drive the architecture and make sure that architects, but also CIOs and IT managers don't lose themselves in the details of the technology. It's crucial to keep the focus on the value and not on the technology itself. IT should serve a business function. IT that doesn't do that is not adding value to the business – it's only there for the sake of technology. The focus must be on improving business as a whole. The four models that we use for this are as follows:

- The **service model**: A business typically maintains a portfolio of services to their customers: selling, aftermarket service, incident, and complaint handling, just to name a few. The service model defines how these services are managed, related to the portfolio of an enterprise. The model itself describes how services are delivered and, more important, how they interact with the customers.

  Examples are self-service and managed service. These two models differ a great deal: self-service allows customers to get services themselves, where in managed services the enterprise takes care of everything, preferably proactively using monitoring. But there are a lot of varieties to the theme. Think of on-demand, personalized, customized, and even fully bespoke services where a service is completely designed and offer to the requirements of the customer.

Every service model comes with specifics to how an enterprise must implement processes to deliver the services according to the model. It also immediately impacts the business model. With a highly standardized service model that can be automated to a large extent, the upfront investments to automate will be high, but managing the service might be very cost-effective due to the automation. With customizable or even complete bespoke service offerings, the amount of labor will per default remain high, with corresponding costs and thus a higher price – at least, when the enterprise still wants to earn some money. The choice of the service model is therefore crucial and the starting point for creating value and defining EA.

In essence, the service model consists of eight domains, as shown in Figure 2-3.

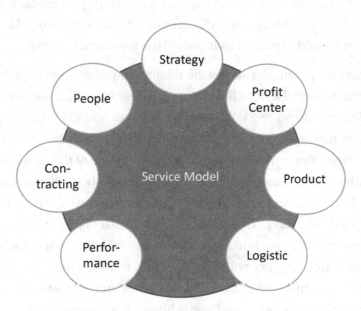

Figure 2-3. *The domains in the service model*

- The **information model**: Whatever the service model is, the enterprise will need IT to support it. To operate IT in a way that it supports the services and with that creates value, we must define what information we need and how we optimize our IT in the value chain and delivery of services. In a self-service model, the customer needs access to the service, for instance, through a web portal or an app. This portal or app must be operated, and to enable IT to a good job, the operators need information on how the portal or app is used.

  That's just a simple example, but we need information in every domain of the service model. We need information – be aware that an information model is not the same as a data model – on the logistic processes and that data must correspond with the contracts that the enterprise has. If the company has a service model that entails the strategy of 7/24 delivery, we need logistic processes that can cater for that, but we also need contracts with logistic partners where the 7/24 is contractually agreed upon. IT systems need to capture data that tells us how well the enterprise is doing and how systems can support the various processes. You could think of a system that facilitates the logistics planning. How a system should capture this is part of the functional model.

  The information model shows the relationships between objects – or artifacts – and the data flow between these objects. If we need to deliver a product to a customer, we need an address and likely a contact method to reach that customer. The information model for the customer now has three objects: the name of the customer, the address of the customer, and the contact method. We can next expand the information model by linking this to the information model of the delivery. That model might consist of method of delivery and delivery time. The two models combine will tell when how and when delivery will take place and to what customer, specified by name and address. In case of an incident, we can even reach the customer and notify him or her. A simplified information model is shown in Figure 2-4.

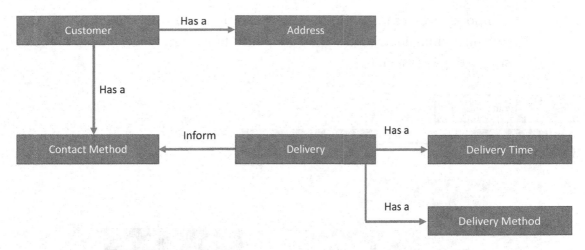

Figure 2-4. *Simplified information model*

- The **functional model**: We have defined what information we need to operate the enterprise. Next, we must define the systems to process that information. We need a model that represents the functions of an enterprise: activities, processes, and operations. The functional model tells us how the enterprise operates. The starting point for the functional model is the business functional model. That model shows the processes that are required to produce a product or a service, from beginning to the end. The model contains all activities that are needed to fulfill that chain.

  Business process modelling is used to define the models. It describes the process including all activities to transform input to output. These models can become very complex, as they start with the requirements (input) and represent all activity to eventually create the output (product or service). The activities form a functional decomposition to which IT systems are designed that support that activity. The model also shows the flow between the activities and thus the interaction between system components.

  To recap, a business has functions to produce a product or a service. These functions are represented in a business functional model. The business functions are then mapped to system components that support the business functions. Figure 2-5 shows a business functional model and a simplified functional model for supporting IT systems.

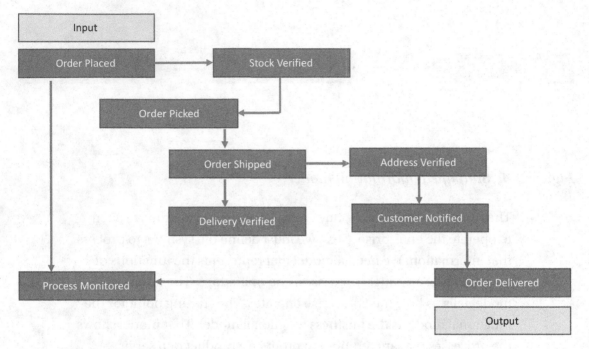

Figure 2-5. *Simplified functional model*

- The **integration model**: In discussing the information model, we noticed that models interact. The integration model shows how processes, information, and systems work together to deliver the value. This is likely the most complex model since it must represent all relationships between business processes and the supporting systems. The challenge here is that first of all business processes will change over time and thus the supporting systems will have to change with it. Besides, systems on themselves have a lifecycle and a change to a system component can influence the business process. The integration model must address this. Important aspects of the model are risk and change management, making sure that the integration is continuously verified and validated.

It demands a comprehensible decomposition of the architecture. The impact of a change should immediately be visible from the architecture. A popular model to work with is the architecture Vee model, used in the Systems Engineering Body of Knowledge (SEBok). The Vee model is shown in Figure 2-6.

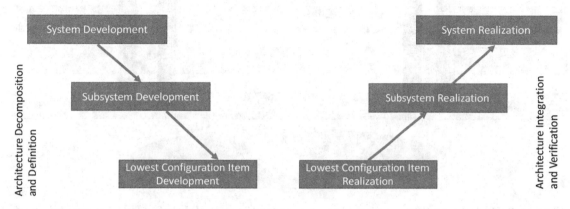

Figure 2-6. *The SEBok Vee model*

The model shows the architecture decomposition and the realization of the system. The decomposition must match the business processes and the functional model.

With these models in place, we have a solid foundation to define the IT value chain as IT4IT describes.

- The business has a mission and a plan, structured in a portfolio.

- Using the information model and the functional model, the business knows what systems it needs to support the business processes and functions.

- Using the service model, the business knows how to deliver products and services to its customers.

- Using the integration model, the business has risk and change management in place and knows how to operate the systems that support the business functions.

It's shown in Figure 2-7.

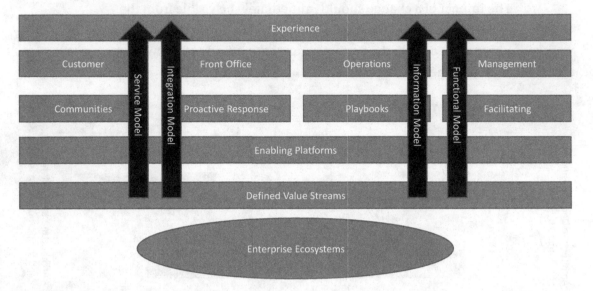

Figure 2-7. *Integrating service model, integration model, information model, and functional model with enterprise layers*

We are using IT4IT as the digital blueprint for our enterprise. We can map the value streams to the enterprise layer model that we presented in the first section of this chapter.

Now we must shape – or reshape – the organization to the value streams. In the section "Defining a Target Architecture and Operating Model," we will discuss this extensively, but it's good to mention here that next to the models that we discussed, we should include an organization and a change model – it's crucial for the business transformation.

We will see in the coming sections that modern enterprises have adopted the concept of shift-left and are decomposing the business into functions and supporting systems, using a microservices architecture to enable flexibility and agility and to make sure that customer demands can be addressed quickly. What IT4IT doesn't do – at least, not initially – is prescribing how the enterprise should organize itself to implement the various models and fulfill the value streams.

A lot of companies implement shift-left by forming small teams to deliver a business function, working according to scrum: small teams, working agile, in short cycles on a very specific set of tasks. The big mistake enterprises make is that these scrum teams still operate as the old business departments in the enterprise. This is known as Conway's law that we quote here: "any organization that designs a system (defined broadly) will produce a design whose structure is a copy of the organization's communication structure."

An organizational change in which entire departments are split into small scrum teams with their own responsibility for a part of the total solution is not an easy task. The total solution is often split into modalities, but this modularity has come to conform to the departmental boundaries that existed before the restructuring. After the formation of the scrum teams, there is an enormous task to divide the often monolithic solution into the responsibilities of the teams. For the time being, the teams have been ordered to work together to realize a refactoring program to divide the product, for instance, software, into independent modules with well-defined interfaces. In many cases it will turn out that this means that the product has to be set up again. This is not the right order, at least not when we really want to transform the enterprise. The likely outcome of this process is creation of legacy and technical debt, but no changes to the organization. The enterprise will still be centered around the products, but not around the customer. Hence, we need a different model to structure our modern enterprise. Basically, we need to define the modern EA from the ground up, as it were completely greenfield, starting with the definition of the value streams, the required business capabilities, and functions mapped to the customer journey.

Before we do that and connect the value streams to the enterprise organization, we should spend some time in studying techniques and tools. That's the topic of the next section.

Using Modern EA Techniques and Tools

In the previous section, we discussed IT4IT intensively and learned how to connect IT with business value streams. We saw that IT4IT addresses the digitization of the enterprise. However, it does not address the shape of the enterprise itself and HOW it should do business. It merely shows how IT can support in digital transformation, but business transformation is a different ballgame. For business transformation we must create a new target operating model for our modern enterprise. That's one of the most important tasks of enterprise architect.

The next challenge is how to create and manage a modern EA that supports that target operating model. As we have seen in Chapter 1, we can use different EA frameworks for this. The Open Group recently released TOGAF 10 that now supports agile organizations and digital transformation through a stronger modularity. Yet, the original steps in TOGAF including the Architecture Development Method (ADM) that we discussed in Chapter 1 are very valid. Most important, TOGAF always starts with the business vision and that's how it should be done.

The Open Agile Architecture (O-AA) takes it a few steps further. O-AA works with building blocks that are very useful. It starts with the agile strategy and next dives into the agile organization and the experience design, before going into the value stream mapping. For the experience design, it quotes Theodor Levitt in his *Marketing Myopia*: "The organization must learn to think of itself not as producing goods or services but as buying customers, as doing the things that will make people want to do business with it." Next, it describes how solution ideas constantly follow customer research in subsequent iterations, leading to value propositions and the corresponding product features. The experience design approach in O-AA is shown in Figure 2-8.

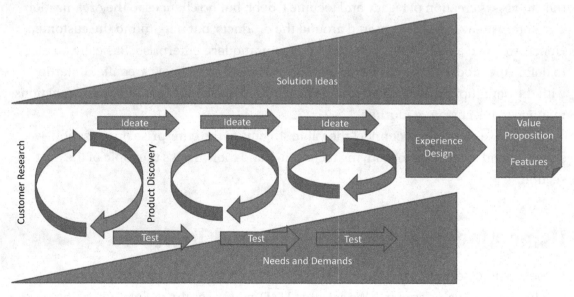

Figure 2-8. *Experience design approach in O-AA*

Both TOGAF 10 and O-AA are more modular and support shifting responsibilities and capabilities to the business. It's already working toward the use of microservices and micro-enterprises to increase agility.

So, we have our frameworks and we know where our enterprise is moving toward. We might have defined our North Star that we discussed in Chapter 1. The actual transformation can start. That transformation will inevitably inflict risks and a lot of hurdles that we need to overcome. As architects, we will be faced with legacy, technical debt, organizational structures that will not function in a modern enterprise, and worst of all, we will be confronted by people in the organization who will not feel the need for the transformation or recognize the value chains. They will not see or understand the need for agility and rearchitecting the enterprise. This in itself is an inhibition point, as we have seen in Chapter 1 when we discussed the ecocycles. An important part of the transformation is to find ways to deal with this inhibition. It's one of the first tasks of the enterprise architect. Most of their work will be about communication. In the final chapter of this book, we will look more closely to the changing role of the architects, since that role is changing. So-called soft skills are getting more important in the role.

Where do we start? The answer is a typical consultants' answer: with an assessment. You have to know where you're coming from to know where you're going to. The assessment is the first technique to use in a transformation. The architect creates a structured inventory of all assets in the enterprise. Again, that's not about technology. The architect starts with the propositions of the enterprise: the products and services that are delivered to customer. From there, the architect drills down to the capabilities of the business or business units, the applications that these businesses use, the data, and lastly the technology. The architect should be able to link all these components: technology, data, and applications must be linked to the propositions. If components can't be mapped to a business capability or a proposition, it has no value.

Since our North Star is likely involving the digital transformation of the enterprise, shouldn't IT be an important component of this assessment? Yes, but not as a starting point. During the assessment, we must look at how IT is supporting our business capabilities (*Business Value Assessment of IT Investments* by Magnus Gammelgard, 2007, Royal Institute of Technology, Stockholm):

- **Data quality**: Data must be accurate, complete, and available.

- **Functional fit**: Ideally there shouldn't be a gap between the business functions and the supporting IT functions. Every IT function and corresponding system must support a business function and capability.

- **Information security**: Data and systems must be protected from unauthorized access and safeguard integrity of data, systems, and thus protect business intelligence.

- **Interoperability**: Systems must be able to exchange information, within the enterprise and the ecosystem where the enterprise is part of.

- **Modifiability**: Systems must be able to adapt to and adopt changes, because of changes in business capabilities and propositions.

- **Performance**: Systems and with that business must be able to respond in a timely manner, corresponding with the requirements of the customers.

- **Safety**: Systems and with that business should not cause any form of risk, danger, or damage to customers. This includes data loss and the consequences of such an event.

- **Usability**: Systems should be easy to use, both for employees and for customers. Ease of use of systems also defines ease of doing business with an enterprise and largely impacts the whole experience of a customer. A very good and very recent example to illustrate this is Twitter and Mastodon. Twitter is extremely easy to use: all you need is an account. When Elon Musk bought the platform late 2022, some users moved to Mastodon, which is a Twitter-alike service, but not as easy to use as Twitter itself. With Mastodon the user also has to choose a specific server, allowing to "host" your own network. Setting up a Mastodon account is simply more work. Even though Twitter lost a number of users, Mastodon will likely not become as popular as Twitter.

Let's take a simple database as an example to apply these principles. The data in the database must be accessible, accurate, and protected from unauthorized usage. The database itself must be able to connect to data sources and systems that can analyze and present data; hence, the database must be interoperable. When required by the business, the database must be modifiable to allow for extra sets of information. This is a very simple example, but it shows that the principles can be applied to all systems and on all levels.

The assessment will highlight the challenges of the business and the gaps between business functions and IT. Business capabilities might be poorly supported or not at all. This will impact the enterprise mission. A proper assessment will also translate these gaps into financial consequences, which can be severe. The enterprise architect plays the key role to identify the gaps, explore the (potential) business risks, and most important, guide in finding solutions to bridge the gaps and steer the transformation of the enterprise.

The enterprise needs to create a vision of their target operating model, supported by digital tools. But before we get to the tools, we need a technology strategy that "matches" the business strategy. In a very simple example, if the business strategy includes the sale through an app, then we need technology that supports building and managing such an app. That's not all, though. If we have an app, then we need to get the app published in stores or providers, for instance, Apple and Android. Publishing an app comes with regulations, compliance, and contracts. The app must be supported, addressing, for instance, scalability and security. Last, we need to figure out how we earn money with the app and the services that we deliver through that app. Then we also need to know what our costs will be in developing and maintaining the app. Without a proper technology strategy, our business strategy will not be fulfilled.

To complete it, the enterprise needs to move fast. Customer behavior – the patterns – change all the time. Our development teams need to capture the feedback from the customer and continuously integrate that feedback into the products and services.

To put it short, a modern EA also embraces and facilitates DevOps, SecOps, and FinOps:

- **DevOps**: A combination of dev (development) and ops (operations) is a way of software development in which the development and management activities are linked and closely interrelated with each other. This requires coordination and collaboration between different disciplines that were previously separated and isolated. Quality controls and security teams are also part of the wider team in the DevOps model.

- **SecOps**: A combination of security and operations. SecOps monitors and continuously assesses risks, aiming to protecting the assets of the enterprise. SecOps teams often operate from a security operations center (SOC). SecOps gets more and more integrated in DevOps, leading to DevSecOps. The idea is that security operations already start with the development of the software, up until the point where the software is released and deployed.

- **FinOps:** A combination of finance and operations. Modern enterprises often use cloud services from big public cloud providers such as Azure, AWS, and Google Cloud. These cloud providers offer services against various payment models, such as pay as you go, on demand, or "reserved" where services are leased for a longer period. Services have various price tags that make it complex to keep track of costs. FinOps offers practices to help keeping control of the use of technology.

These processes must be integrated in the EA of the modern, transformed, and digital enterprise, making EA a complex effort. We must find ways to manage this complexity. In the next section we will learn how we can manage this.

Managing Enterprise Architecture

Finally, we get to a point where we're going to talk about tools – a bit. We need tools to help us in managing EA. As EA is integrating IT with business processes and also needs to support agile processes in modern enterprises, we can't simply rely on just ArchiMate and Visio anymore. EA has become complex and agile, so we need tools that can capture both IT and business and keep track of all assets.

Enterprise architecture management is a relative new domain. It aims to support capturing and structuring the mapping of business processes, capabilities, and propositions to supporting technology. It must enable the continuous analysis of business, information, and technology against the enterprise strategy. The outcomes of the analysis must support the strategy or point exactly to where gaps are, for instance, by indicating that specific technology is not supporting a business capability and should be suspended.

Cost analysis is an important process in enterprise architecture management. A full inventory of technology – applications and infrastructure – represents costs. These costs are part of the total cost of ownership (TCO). The TCO is the total cost for purchasing and owning technology during its entire lifecycle. All costs must be included from the moment of purchase until the moment the enterprise disposes of it.

The next thing that we must analyze is the return on investment (ROI). ROI indicates the return on investments – what has been left over from the investments that the enterprise has made or what the losses have been lost on the investments. It all adds up to the business case: What investments does the enterprise have to make and how will it fulfill the need of the customer? Business case and business strategy obviously are very closely related. At the end of the day, the enterprise needs to make money. Otherwise, it will be very short-lived.

It requires that the enterprise architect has to think of every single aspect of the enterprise: the strategy, the business case, business capabilities, mapping of capabilities to technology, TCO, and ROI. This is required to support strategic decision-making.

Part of the enterprise architecture management is application portfolio management. Business capabilities are mapped to functionality and next to supporting applications. A complete, accurate list of all applications in use, including a functional mapping, must be available and managed. In the world of the modern enterprise where teams work in DevOps structures with software pipelines, continuous integration/continuous deployment (CI/CD), and microservices, applications will change fast. Application portfolio management has become essential. Changes of, for instance, software versions and the underlying infrastructure that is more and more used from cloud technology will directly impact the function of the business and might even lead to risks.

We promised that we would talk about tools. There are several tools that can capture the EA and match this to business processes and capabilities. Examples are LeanIX, Ardoq, ServiceNow, and Software AG Alfabet Cloud. Be aware that this is complex software, and it doesn't release the enterprise architect from the work or the responsibilities. The tools merely help in creating and keeping an overview. There's still a lot to do, starting with creating a target operating model for the modern enterprise. We will talk about that in the next section.

Defining a Target Architecture and Operating Model

Before we discuss a target operating model or the target enterprise model, we must define why we need a different model. The common answer to that question is digital transformation. A better answer might be business transformation. The reason to do that is because otherwise we won't elevate – or perhaps detach is a better word – EA from technology. If we talk "digital," we talk technology and we extensively discussed that EA is not about technology in the first place. Technology is an enabler and yet, as we have seen, without technology a lot of modern businesses wouldn't even exist today.

EA should care about business transformation. The reasons to execute business transformation can be

- Increasing revenue

- Increasing market share by exploring new market segments

- Improving customer satisfaction, by enhancing their experience

- Cutting costs

We should add one more to this list: to embed the customer. Our new target model will enable the customer-driven enterprise. We need business transformation to achieve this by restructuring the organization, the business portfolio, the business capabilities, and eventually the technology the organization uses. It means that organizations must go through a number of stages or phases during the transformation.

1. Recognize the need for change.

2. Convince stakeholders that the change is needed to stay relevant.

3. Explore and agree the shape of the change, including objectives of the change.

4. Assess the current situation of the organization and how change will impact the organization.

5. Design the new organization.

6. Implement the new organization.

7. Evaluate and adjust.

Let there be no misunderstanding: this is a continuous process and certainly not a one-time off. During the transformation, the organization will recognize new opportunities and develop new competencies, leading to new changes.

How do we transform a business? Most businesses come from a traditional seller model as a seller-driven enterprise. The strategy of these enterprises is to maximize product profitability. The seller-driven enterprise is characterized by the following parameters:

- **A singular customer offering**: "one size fits all," no customization

- **The channels are product driven**: All marketing is centered around the product. What can it do, what are the specs, and what does the customer need to do to use the product?

- The organization is functionally siloed.

The enterprise is completely focused on push, in all its activities.

Outtasking and outsourcing have gradually become very popular models to manage these enterprises. The enterprise itself is completely focused on growth through selling from a push strategy and maximizing the profitability. One way to do that is by heavily cutting costs. Outsourcing and outtasking of noncore activities can actually bring down costs. But there's a risky downside to this model in a world where customer demand is changing rapidly. The outsourced tasks are not customer focused but cost focused. These tasks are captured in strict contracts with service-level agreements that are hard to change. As the enterprise is confronted with the changing demands at high pace, it also needs to adapt these contracts with its suppliers. The Voice of the Customer must be distributed throughout the entire delivery chain.

Sometimes a shock to the system reveals the weaknesses of the model in a dramatic way. For example, during the COVID pandemic a lot of countries issued travel bans, leaving airports as good as empty. Airports typically have outsourced activities to third-party companies. Think of security staff, cleaners, and luggage handlers. Delivering companies were faced with high costs because of inactive staff and a lot of people were laid off. They could still fulfill the contracts with the airport. When the world opened again and people started traveling, airports found themselves in a situation where these third-party companies could not scale up services fast enough anymore, leading to chaos on a number of airports.

Now, a pandemic is an extraordinary situation, but the problems did show that a seller-driven enterprise has a hard time to survive in today's business. Some enterprises have adopted the customer-centric way of thinking. These enterprises focus on segments of customers and are organized in segments, meaning that not every function is siloed but grouped as a segment delivering a product or a service to a defined segment of customers. There's interaction between the segments, but it's still not agile enough to address changing demands at a high pace.

Now, let's look at a modern enterprise. The modern enterprise is customer-driven. It's characterized by

- Pull (collaboration)

- Interactive and proactive

- Integrated, seamless interoperable working micro-enterprises

- Focused on customer outcome

The modern enterprise addresses the five parameters that we discussed in the first section of this chapter: product, perspective, patterns, platforms, and promotor score. These are the key performance indicators that must be enabled by the EA. The responsibilities to achieve these KPIs are in the business, so the architecture should facilitate this by allowing for shift-left. DevOps, SecOps, and FinOps must be included in the architecture by promoting an agile operating model. Micro-enterprises are an organizational model that facilitates this. We will discuss this further, but first we need to do some decomposing of enterprise functions using the five KPIs for the modern enterprise. In the section about IT4IT, we learned that decomposition is essential to eventually create a target operating model.

Our target operating model embraces shift-left, embeds the customer, and is event-driven so that the customer gets the service they need, at the right time and the right place. To create agility, we need a microservices architecture and a corresponding organization with micro-enterprises. Let's make this a bit more tangible in an example. It's very important to remember that everything an enterprise does must create value. The enterprise creates value by delivering a good experience. Hence, we are architecting for experience and embedding the customer. Second thing to remember is that an enterprise never stands on its own: it's part of an ecosystem. So, our business decomposition is always a decomposition in services that are delivered from various entities in that ecosystem. Our architecture must reflect this. Basically, our architecture must reflect the customer journey.

Once more we will study the process of traveling, but this time by indicating the value streams.

Booking a travel is a trigger that sets a number of actions in motion. First, the traveler visits a website of a travel agency. The agency has a portfolio of destinations and ways of traveling. It has agreements with hotels and airlines to enable the offerings. The traveler sets his destination and books the hotel and flight. The travel agency checks the availability of the hotel and the airline. The hotel and airline send back the confirmation and subsequently the travel agency forwards this confirmation to the traveler.

The next step is the payment. The agency sends a bill to the traveler and offers a variety of options to pay for the expenses. The traveler uses a credit card. The payment is submitted, and the credit card company checks the credibility of the customer. That's send to the agency and the payment is fulfilled. Now the entire travel has been planned. The travel agency sends the vouchers and the airline tickets.

The traveler arrives at the airport where they check in their luggage and proceed to the security checks and customs. They might do some shopping in the tax-free zone and buy a last coffee at Starbucks before they take a seat in the waiting area until the boarding begins. While they wait, they check the details of the hotel in the booking app.

At this stage, the traveler has worked with at least a handful of companies, if not more: the agency, the airline, the airport, some shops, security staff, and the hotel. Likely, services have been outsourced, so the number of companies that our traveler has to deal with is much bigger. All these companies define the value stream and the experience of the traveler. There's only one way to architect the value stream and that's by taking the perspective of the traveler, embedding the customer. We will have to treat every service as a microservice that can be adapted to the needs of the customer quickly. We need organizations that can build, deploy, and manage these services, interacting with other services.

The challenge for the architect is to visualize the journey, identify the services and the interactions, and map these to relevant technologies that support these services, providing the desired experience for the customer. We'll do that in the next section.

Mapping the Customer Journey

Where do we start? Keep in mind that we are following the customer on a journey and that we work on an architecture that aims to provide a good experience.

A customer value map is a good starting point.

- The organization has collected the specific customer requirements and needs to map these to the business capabilities. These capabilities must be aligned with the business strategy of the enterprise.

- The capabilities are captured in the business portfolio, containing propositions.

- These propositions – products and services – now must be mapped to the needs of the customers, covering the desired features, and clearly showing the benefits to the customers.

- That forms the value proposition: the benefits a product and/or service will have once delivered to the customer.

- The service model is very important in the delivery of the value proposition. It's not solely the product or service itself that represents value, but also the way how it's delivered to the customer.

It's very plausible that an enterprise has to serve different groups of customers, or customer personas. The propositions must target the right persona, using the various models that we discussed. There might be a group of customers that wants to purchase a product in a real shop, other customers might want to order the same product through the Internet. That defines the service model. But also, the product or service itself might differ per persona. That will impact the organization of the enterprise. If we want to embed the customer, we must tailor the enterprise to the various customer personas, executing and delivering the propositions to the needs of these personas.

The next task for the architect is to define the value stream. Basically, it means that we must set out and detail the various steps the customer must follow to get the value of the product or a service. That defines how the product or service must be delivered to the customer. Let's use our travel example one more time to define a value stream for booking a flight, starting with the process as shown in Figure 2-9.

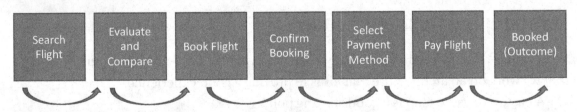

Figure 2-9. *Value stream example for booking a flight*

It gets interesting from this point, since you can imagine that we should define value streams for every product or service that forms the total experience for the customer. That might include booking extra services such as a hotel, reflected in Figure 2-10.

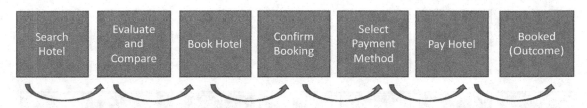

Figure 2-10. *Value stream example for booking a hotel*

In the integrated value stream, delivering value to the customer might look like the process in Figure 2-11.

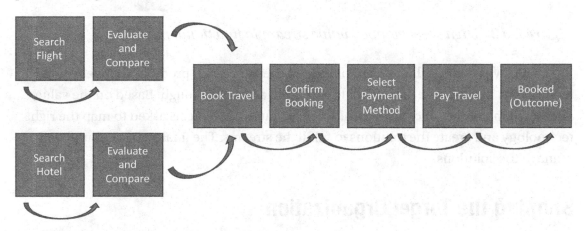

Figure 2-11. *Integrated value stream example for booking travel*

This is where microservices come in: we can dynamically scale the required services at the desired time and place – and even in the desired format.

First, we need to map the value stream to the functional model. It's shown at a high level in Figure 2-12.

Figure 2-12. *High-level mapped value stream to functional model*

Lastly, we can map this to technology and even to certain products that deliver that technology. This is more the role for the solution architect, though. Based on the value streams, capabilities, and the propositions, a solution architect is asked to map the right technology and create the solutions to fulfill the streams. The final step is to build and manage the solutions.

Shaping the Target Organization

The following chapter will be all about the organizational model and how we transform the enterprise itself, since most enterprises will not be born in the digital era and have to deal with quite some legacy. Still, we can transform these enterprises and even shape them into responsive, agile micro-enterprises that are close to the customer.

In this section we will briefly introduce the micro-enterprises as an organizational model that fits the delivery of microservices and enables the embedding of the customer by practicing a true shift-left mentality. The architecture of the customer value streams and the organization model together form the target operating model.

We discussed Conway's law that essentially tells that organizations keep holding on to the old organizational forms, even when the value streams and corresponding delivery models change. If we transform to microservices, we must transform the organization with it. An organizational model that fits this principle is Rendanheyi that transforms the organization into micro-enterprises that are really close to the customer.

The model was invented by Zhang Ruimin, CEO of one of China's largest manufacturers called Haier. He transformed the traditional organization to a network organization, consisting of small entities – indeed, micro-enterprises.

Rendanheyi means employee–user combination. There's a direct connection between the employee of the enterprise and the user, the customer. The employee listens to the customer, where in a traditional organization the employee typically follows orders from management. The customer is at the center of every decision. According to Ruimin, it's the only way to stay relevant. To achieve this, the Rendanheyi model is built on three pillars: (1) a platform organization, (2) personalized user experience, and (3) shift from employees to entrepreneurs. These are explained in the following texts:

- The **platform organization**: Rendanheyi promotes the platform organization. Due to the Internet, competition will not be between enterprises, but between platforms. Enterprises therefore need to reshape themselves as platforms, consisting of micro-enterprises and behaving as an ecosystem. The market, the customer demand, drives these micro-enterprises that act autonomously, continuously being in contact with their customers.

- **Personalized user experience**: Throughout this chapter we used the terms customer and user as synonyms. In Rendanheyi, however, there's a huge difference between the two. Customers buy something once, where users are continuously interacting (pattern) with the product or service. That defines the experience. Products should not just be of good quality, but deliver an experience. Since users are continuously interacting, the micro-enterprises need to be in constant contact with the users, aiming to not only sell products but to deliver and improve the experience.

- **Shift from employees to entrepreneurs**: Employees simply do as they're told; entrepreneurs are driven by the user who is in the center of the model. Rendanheyi is about the embedded customer. Entrepreneurs get paid on the basis of the value they deliver to their users. If users don't recognize that value anymore, the micro-enterprise is not innovating and likely not listening to the user. The hard consequence of this model is that entrepreneurs will have to leave. Be aware that Rendanheyi doesn't have leaders: it's about self-organization and self-motivation, directly coming from the users.

Sounds drastic? Indeed, and the model might not fit every enterprise. It's a bold and a highly disrupting move, but a number of modern enterprises have proven already that it works. The logical following question then is, how can an enterprise make this work? How do we make these micro-enterprises successful and empower them to overcome inhibitions? To answer that question, we need to look at the four zones model by Geoffrey A. Moore. The four zones are shown in Figure 2-13.

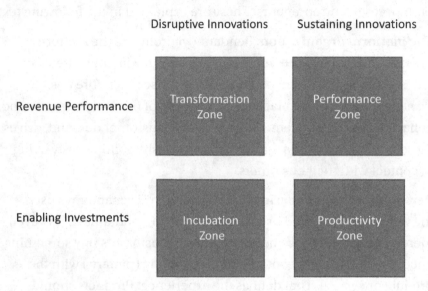

Figure 2-13. *The four zones by Geoffrey A. Moore*

In this model we have to start at the performance zone and then rotate clockwise. Both the performance zone and the productivity zone are the zones where most traditional organizations are focusing on the ROI – the return on investment. The zones are aiming for sustainment. The organizations are typically seller-driven; that's their operating model. The big risk here is that enterprises will be disrupted from the outside. It might either take a lot of efforts – and investments – to change the organization then or it might be simply too late, causing these enterprises to miss the next wave, as Moore formulates it.

The next two zones are the disruptive zones. In the incubation zone, new markets are explored and value propositions defined to target these markets. The propositions might not generate revenue at this stage; the zone is purely intended to prepare the enterprise for the "next big thing" and to stay relevant. In the transformation zone, these propositions are scaled and the enterprise will start to gain revenue. But from the transformation zone, it will enter the performance zone again. The model of the four zones implicitly shows that enterprises must continuously disrupt themselves, to avoid from being disrupted. Since it's very hard, if not impossible, to apply this to large, monolithic-driven enterprises, we must unbundle the organization into agile units and rebundle them in delivering value streams.

The next chapter will be all about the process of this unbundling and rebundling and why this is an important task for the enterprise architect.

Applying Best Practices

So far, we discussed the principles of embedding the customer, defining the customer journey, the value streams, and organizing the enterprise around these value streams. In the last section we discussed that no enterprise would escape the call for disruption. Either they adopt a model in which the organization continuously disrupts itself or it gets disrupted from the outside. The enterprise architect plays a crucial role in keeping the enterprise on track by shaping models to get to value propositions and make sure the enterprise remains relevant in its business domain.

That's easier said than done. The final chapter of this book will be about the role of the enterprise architect, but we can already state that this role is changing dramatically. Their role is to understand complex changes and find ways to control these changes. McKinsey has listed some best practices to execute EA, among others:

- **Involve executives in key decisions**: This may sound as very obvious, but it also means that the enterprise architect must be part of the executive board. EA is about setting the strategy and making sure that the strategy is implemented through business capabilities, business structures, and organization.

- **Focus on the business outcome**: One more time, every business should add value. It must focus on the outcome that the customer is perceiving. If that outcome is achieved, the business outcome will be achieved.

- **Be clear on the strategic planning**: That's what EA should do, instead of getting caught up in daily, operational problems. EA must focus on the business strategy, planning, and portfolio. These must be aligned with strategic resource planning that includes staff and material resources.

I'm adding these two practices since they have showed to bring value to understand and execute change.

- **Include culture**: Every enterprise has a certain mindset. Validate whether that mindset is allowing for change or forming an inhibition. Later in this book I will extensively discuss the growth mindset that the modern enterprise needs – and all its stakeholders.

- **Create a change plan**: The change plan should be looking at people first. Change is coming from people. They must adopt and embrace change.

Still, we can add one more practice: get out and play. What we mean with that is don't start working on EA in isolation. In Chapter 1 we discussed the House of Quality (HoQ) and the Voice of the Customer (VoC). An important process in both HoQ and VoC is the Gemba walk. Enterprise architects should do the Gemba walk, invented by Taiichi Ohno, a Japanese engineer who created the Toyota Production System. The idea is simple but absolutely a best practice: visit the workplace that you want to improve and see for yourself how the work is done. Take a look and then ask why it's done in this way.

It's important to define the relation with the VoC.

- Does the way of working guarantee that the customer needs and requirements are being met?

- Are processes leading to the desired output as we have defined in the planning and design phase of HoQ?

- If not, what can be improved?

Listen to the employees, create mock-ups, and test these in simulations with the employees. Again, this is a continuous process. All to get to the best value for the customer. This is an impactful, intensive process, especially for traditionally organized enterprises. Let's call these enterprises earth-born, on their way to a more modern, digital, constant changing world. They are earth-born migrants and we'll learn more about them in the next chapter.

Summary

This was an important chapter. We discussed how we can transform an enterprise from a seller-driven to customer-driven organization. First, we discussed new thinking parameters where we explored how customers change the enterprise not only through continuously changing demands for product and service features, but also in the way how they purchase these products and services. We learned that platforms have become very important for modern enterprises. We concluded that experience is the key driver for customers and that we need to capture this in value streams delivering that experience.

Since the modern enterprise is digitizing, we need to map these value streams to supporting IT systems. We learned how IT4IT can help us with that. However, the customer experience is always leading. The enterprise architect has an important role to shape the business portfolio, capabilities, and functions to match the steps in the customer journey. This includes unbundling and rebundling the organization into micro-enterprises that are close to the customer and capable of agile, fast response to changing needs. We talked about Rendanheyi as a possible organizational model for the modern enterprise. In the final section of this chapter, we studied best practices that can help the enterprise architect to find solutions that enable the enterprise to stay relevant in its business domain. In the next chapter, we will dive further into the transformation of the enterprise itself.

CHAPTER 3

The Real World of Digital Transformation

How do earth-born (traditional) companies start the journey to become modern companies using scalable cloud-native technology, agile frameworks, and DevOps? What are the modern business challenges and how can EA address these? In this chapter we will start this journey, explaining the challenges and the forthcoming steps that the enterprise must take in order to adopt the change. We will work on a new target operating model and a roadmap to implement this model, by looking at transforming the organization itself in micro-enterprises and applying architecture rules to the new digital systems of the organization. Transformation means change and change inevitably comes with risks; hence, we will also address risk management in this chapter.

The Challenge of the Earth-Born Enterprise

The first time I heard about the earth-born enterprise was probably at a convention. At first, I thought it was referring to the sustainability program of a company, but then I realized that it meant something else. Earth-born companies were traditional companies that started their journey to the cloud. They had become earth-born migrants. I like the analogy so much that I decided to use it myself to point out the challenges that these traditional companies have in migrating to the cloud – better said, the challenges they face in their digital transformation.

One more time and because we can't stress this enough, digital transformation is not solely about technology or cloud. These are merely tools. The enterprise itself must transform, must change. Change comes with inhibition, with setbacks, with mistakes and continuous improvement. Be aware that the word failure hasn't been mentioned. There's no such thing as failure unless the enterprise stops the change completely. When it has failed and once it has stopped changing and transforming, it will never recover again.

© Jeroen Mulder 2023
J. Mulder, *Modern Enterprise Architecture*, https://doi.org/10.1007/978-1-4842-9066-8_3

That's probably the biggest challenge the traditional enterprise faces: keeping the change alive. Keeping momentum. But first, what characterizes a traditional company? It's not the products it makes, it's the mentality of such an enterprise. Thinking that they will stay relevant at all times is their greatest inhibition point. Usually, it's caused by a lack of strategic vision and the immutable faith that they deliver a unique product or service. Or because the enterprise holds a very strong position in their markets. None of this ensures that enterprises will stay relevant; they all will face change at some point in time. That often means that a business model will have to change.

In Chapter 2 we discussed the manufacturing of tires. That's a perfect example of a changing, traditional business. The transformation of that business was skyrocketed through the COVID pandemic. Less traveling meant less car mileages and thus less need for new tires. Companies reworked their business models and adopted subscriptions with services, offered through apps and vehicle tracking technology. Where in the old model data was collected when tires were replaced at a dealer or garage, now data could be collected continuously, telling the manufacturer exactly how fast and under what conditions a tire performs best or wears out. It was the innovation from the racetracks that found its way to the consumer market. The subscription was the add-on to make it really interesting for the customers.

The business model as such has got nothing to do with technology. The model is supported by technology, which is a different thing. But it takes a strategic vision to change the business model. The next stop is the enterprise architect to incorporate the new model and create the architecture supporting the model.

Let's take a look at another business that is impacting every single human being: healthcare. That's at its very heart a very traditional business model. People get sick and need medical help to fix the health issue. For that, the doctor gets paid, where we skip the fact that there's a complex system of insurances that actually takes care of reimbursements. No one would disagree that healthcare needs to transform as well. Here another driver plays an important role for the need of transformation. Healthcare as such will stay relevant, yet transformation is needed because the global healthcare system simply comes to a halt for a lot of people if changes are not implemented.

In more simple words, we, the customers or the patients, aren't able to afford it any longer. The main reason for this is a growing world population that at the same time gets older. We don't have enough people to take care of this growing and aging population. It's for good reasons that healthcare is one of these businesses that intensively looks at technology that can support in cure and care. Yet, if there's one business that is reluctant in adopting technology, it's probably healthcare. Doctors and nurses want to see and feel the patient. They didn't become medical professionals to sit behind screens, pushing buttons.

Every single business needs to transform, sooner or later. Why doesn't it happen then? The three main reasons are as follows:

- **Lack of resources**, or better lack of skilled resources: We will extensively talk about this in the forthcoming chapters.

- **Unpredictable outcomes**, or nontrusted predictable outcomes: What can we expect from transformation is a good question. But it's often more a matter of perception and looking for proof as an excuse not to start the transformation in the first place.

- **Business cases that aren't justified well enough**: The problem here is that business cases are typically about the money. But a business case encompasses so much more than just the financials. Are we helping our customers better? We might have to invest in improving services that do not directly translate in more profit, but in happier customers. At the end it will definitively translate into revenue and profit.

We can overcome these challenges by setting a clear strategy and taking it all step by step. In the next sections we will discover in what order we must take these steps. Surprise: It starts with the workplace, really.

Starting the Journey: Earth-Born Migrants

Transforming a traditional, earth-born company into a digital-ready enterprise isn't an easy task. But, it's absolutely doable as long as we don't try to do everything at the same time. There are a few ground rules in starting the migration starting with the most important rule: leverage the power of small. It's a cliché, but the easiest step is by digitizing the workplace.

Hold on, where's the part about Voice of the Customer, customer-embedded and adding business value? Is transforming the workplace doing that? What good will it do to the customer when we digitize the workplace? The answer is a lot. When we make work easy, customers can be helped faster and better by happy personnel. In other words, do not underestimate the importance of a proper workplace that enables workers in doing a proper job. It all adds up to the workplace experience.

Fair enough, we won't be changing the business with this. On the other hand, starting the business transformation without good tools is a perfect recipe for total failure. That will be the key message in this section: the order of things.

Again, we start with the workplace and the workplace experience. It's the perfect environment to get used to digital tools and, extremely important, new business models such as software as a service (SaaS). The majority of businesses will transform to a subscription-based business model. Workplace services were and are ahead of the game. The workplace experience helps people to change the mindset about digital. This is something that is well understood by companies such as Apple and Microsoft who integrate services into the workplace, making it easy for people to work on the same documents on various devices, but with the same look and feel, independent of the device. Users can shift between devices so that documents, schedules, and means of communication are available at convenience, independent from place or time.

Remember your first PC? It's very likely that it came with a disk that contained the software to install the operating system and some applications, typically Microsoft Windows and Office. It also came with a 16-digit license key that the user needed to enter at first use. The costs – a one-off purchase – were significant; hence, a lot of illegal copies were distributed. Worse, if you needed or wanted an upgrade, you would have to pay the total fee again – which only a few among did. Admit it, most of us ran outdated versions of software to prevent high purchase costs again and again.

Microsoft changed that model and turned to cloud-based software that was continuously updated and upgraded. The only thing we as user needed to do is get ourselves a subscription to that software. For a few dollars per month, we got ourselves to guarantee of managed, secure software. And Microsoft got itself a business model with guaranteed monthly revenue. It's the ultimate model to embed the customers – or lock in if you want to perceive it from a more negative side. Still, the subscription-based economy holds the future for many enterprises. However, it's a business model that can only be sustained in a digitized enterprise, providing anything as a service. We will learn much more about this. Figure 3-1 shows the basics of the model.

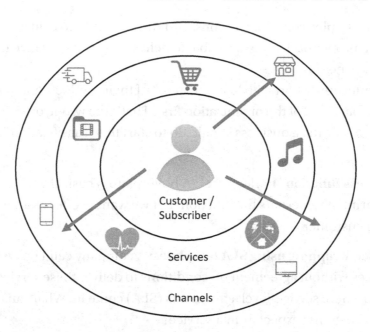

Figure 3-1. *Subscription model as base for SaaS*

The challenge is how to transform your business to enable the adoption of this model. In that model we deliver a product and provide services to use that product in an optimized way, fulfilling customer specifications and needs. Services can be called anytime, anyplace, anywhere. For that we need digital aids, offered in a subscription. The customer pays a small fee per a specified period, entitling to use the service "on demand." This is what we refer to as saasification, although the first s stands for software, the concept is way more generic.

Before we dive into that, it should also be noted that the business model of subscriptions and the derived SaaS is nothing new. It has proven to be a very successful model over many decades. The technology with cloud and digital tools is new, but the principle isn't. Just read *Business Adventures* by John Brooks: in one chapter, he describes the rise of Xerox, who made millions with copiers. Especially the model 914 was their moneymaker. In 1966 companies could buy it for 27,500 USD, but they could also rent it for 25 USD a month, with a minimal of 49 USD worth of copies at 4 cents per copy. This business model was favored by Xerox, since it could make more money through the rental model. Copy as a service, ahead of its time. And what about that service? Well, the machine was so utterly complex that Xerox maintained a staff of thousands of field engineers to keep the machines running, tells Brooks in his book. There might be some similarities to be spotted in our modern age world with cloud native, DevOps, complex code, integrations, and APIs. What Xerox did was making sure that it had a proper backbone to be able to deliver that service, since it knew how complex the machine was.

Too many enterprises start with "saasification" of their products and services without dealing with the back end of the organization first. That's the wrong order.

Let's just look on what a business should do to start this "saasification." It's quite a list.

- **Business function "boilerplate"**: A boilerplate is basically a blueprint. It represents the function that we want to offer as a service to the customer.

- **Service wrapping using SLA templates**: A company can't deliver services without agreement on conditions to deliver these services. That's where service-level agreements (SLA) come in. What can and may a customer expect from a service?

- **Security policies**: Security is not on top of sauce. It's integrated in the service, so that a customer can be sure that the service is developed and deployed according to all relevant security policies and compliancy rules.

- **IAM**: Identity and access management. Who is allowed to do what, when, where, and why? This doesn't only count for human resources, but also for systems and functions of systems. Is a web server allowed to access a specific database?

- **Deployment policies**: How is software and, with that, the application deployed? What must be done to get software running on various devices, providing the same functionality on different devices, with the same level of security and performance? How is the lifecycle per device managed, meaning software on various devices should be on the same level?

- **Monitoring and metering**: Services need to be measured and monitored. Is the service running and, more important, is it running as expected without errors?

- **API definition**: A service or application will likely not run in splendid isolation. It will have to communicate with other services and applications. The communication is regulated in APIs –application programming interfaces. Applications need to speak to same language using a mutually agreed protocol. Therefore, API definition is crucial.

- **CI/CD and "blueprint automation"**: Continuous integration and continuous deployment are terms in DevOps. Digital enterprises need speed: speed of development in new services, speed in deploying these services. Speed requires that developers and operators work closely together to avoid time-consuming handovers and to ensure that applications are built in such way that they can be managed according to the specifications of operations. But speed also requires automation. Humans make mistakes, and for one, human labor is expensive. In automated software pipelines organizations can continuously improve applications and deploy these as soon as they are run to launch into production.

- **Images**: The blueprint for an application and the underlying infrastructure. The latter can be virtual machines or containers hosted in public clouds such as AWS, Azure, or Google Cloud. Infrastructure – computers, storage, and network – needs to be configured in the right way to properly run applications and services.

- **Guardrails**: In essence, rules that keep development teams and with that the enterprise on the right track. In digital environments, these guardrails are often used to check controls, preventive or detective. They go hand in hand with policies and basically check whether environments are set up within the boundaries of the policies.

- **Scanning (SAST/DAST)**: Static application security testing and dynamic application security testing are really the bare necessity in scanning. These scans are used to detect vulnerabilities. However, in DevOps security must be more intensive, including chaos monkey and blue/green line deployments. In blue/green line deployments, organizations run two separated, yet identical environments – one with the current functionality and one with the new, planned functionality. Chaos monkey is used to randomly switch off parts in the environment to test how resilient the environment is.

- **Service provisioning**: This is the actual deployment of the service, including the support that customers can call.

- **Market place**: Once the service and application are ready, an enterprise needs to make it general available. Big – online – marketplaces are a good place. Think of the various app stores.

- **Billing**: Obviously, enterprises need to get paid. Hence, we need a billing mechanism and a system that can handle the billing.

It comes together in Figure 3-2.

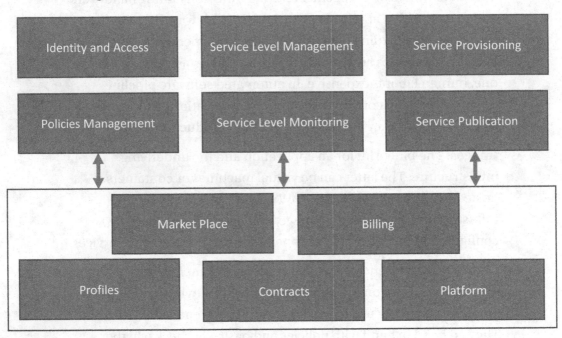

Figure 3-2. *Basic SaaS provisioning model*

So, if a subscription-based business model providing SaaS is the end goal of a digital transformation, then we have to make sure that we're doing things in the right order. It's start with a digital-ready enterprise and that's where EA can be a true guiding light. Let's have a closer look at that specific order:

1. **Workplace**: Get your organization ready for the digital era. Let people get used to subscription-based services and SaaS. The workplace is a great start.

2. **Back end**: The next step is getting the enterprise ready for digitalization. Create and migrate the enterprise's back-end systems to platforms that are scalable and agile, ready to deliver new digital services.

3. **Customer applications from legacy**: Transforming legacy is a very tedious step. Just lift and shift will not provide the foundation to move forward with a digital transformation. A lot of legacy systems are still monolithic and with that not scalable or easy to implement new features. Enterprises will be forced to take bold decisions and start creating architectures with microservices.

4. **Innovations** with among others AI, robotics, blockchain, and Web3.0: Once the core of the enterprise is digitized and ready for digitalization, we can start implementing the real business accelerators with AI-modelling, robotics, deliver-enriched services with augmented and virtual reality, and so forth.

5. **Continuous innovation**: Obviously, it doesn't stop there. It never stops. In a digital-ready enterprise, we have the tools to continuously innovate, create new services for customers, and stay relevant.

There's one thing that should be mentioned here once more: security. Why isn't it mentioned separately? Because it's not something separate. Security is intrinsic on all layers, in every technology, in every business, service, and product by default. Without integrated security, all is lost. Take that last sentence quite literally. It's not a menu out of which enterprises can pick and choose: they either implement security all the way or they don't. There's no in between here.

This order of digitalization is something that has been recognized across the board. Microsoft's CEO Satya Nadella revealed his vision during the 2022 edition of Inspire, demonstrating the digital imperative for every organization. He also distinguishes five key domains:

1. Migrate to cloud (infrastructure)

2. Empower fusion teams

3. Unify data and apply AI models

4. Collaborative business process

5. Prioritize security

They seem different than the ones we discussed before? Not really. Nadella too stresses the need for a sound, solid base infrastructure that teams in enterprises can use to develop new services and products. Innovation is driven by data and AI. These teams must be able to work together in joint collaboration. And of course, security must be top of mind.

These are all parts of the new EA.

Guiding the Transformation from EA

In the previous section, we learned that digital transformation impacts the entire enterprise. It starts with the business demand, but without having a proper digital backbone, enterprises will not succeed in this transformation. We can guide this process from the enterprise architecture. But we need to have a plan.

That plan starts with having a target operating model, or TOM. On a short term, this is the first milestone that the enterprise should accomplish: design and agree upon the TOM. This involves much more than just the technology or tools, as we already concluded in the previous chapters. The TOM comprises

- Strategy

- Vision on the desired operating state

- Processes

- Organization

Defining the TOM means that we implicitly are defining a roadmap for change and a blueprint for our target organization: it's our navigation for the earth-born migration to a new world. To be able to define this roadmap, we first need to know what our current state is, the current operating model. From there we can plan the steps to get to our TOM. Basic steps to do this are as follows:

- **External drivers**: Everything that "forces" the enterprise to change. Typically, these are economic factors, such as changing market conditions, including changing customer demands. A very good example is the car industry: this industry is forced to abandon the traditional engine that runs on fossil fuels and have to switch to electric powered cars. Also, geopolitical factors can play an important role here. Enterprises need to understand and anticipate these external drivers. A way to do this is through a PESTLE Analysis: Political, Economic, Social, Technological, Legal, and Environmental Analysis.

- **Internal drivers**: You need to know where you're coming from to know where you can go. This means that you have to understand the current mode of operations (CMO). Enterprise architects can use SWOT to capture the CMO: strengths, weaknesses, opportunities, and threats. Once we have the CMO, we can define our roadmap to the desired state or the future mode of operations (FMO).

- **Competition analysis**: Where does the enterprise stand in comparison with other competing companies? Don't limit to the main, known competitors, but make sure that startups are captured as well in the analysis. Startups aren't slowed down by legacy and can – they will – move fast, likely disrupting the market. All too often we see traditional companies starting to fight these newbies when they already captured quite some market share. Probably the best example here is Uber. The Uber cars were everywhere when only it was then where the traditional taxi companies started realizing that they needed to act.

- **Vision, culture, and values**: Transformation comes with change and change inevitably comes with a change of culture. If an organization has a very hierarchical structure and now is unbundled and rebundled again in micro-enterprises or starts working in DevOps teams, abandoning the waterfall projects for agile working, this will have a severe impact on the way people do their work. That's the reason why it's crucial to start with the internal organization first. Although it's not the scope of this book, we like to provide the five ground rules for changing an organization:

  1. Keep the strategy simple and comprehensible.

  2. Failures are not a bad thing, as long as they are recognized in an early stage and "fixed."

  3. Leverage the power of small; start with a minimal viable product. This also applies to organizations themselves. Don't try to boil the ocean, but start with small groups.

4. Make sure that every individual in the enterprise understands the urgency to change.

5. Oh – and management: don't isolate yourself, but mingle with the crowds, the workforce. A way to do this is by Gemba walks. Visit the workplace that you want to improve. Today Gemba is part of Six Sigma, but originally it was invented by Taiichi Ohno, learning managers and supervisors to see for themselves how the work is done.

Our roadmap already starts to get a certain shape, identifying three main stages:

- Initiate

- Adopt

- Expand

We will build and further explore this roadmap in the next sections, but first, what are the components that we must take care of in defining the TOM?

We distinguish three tiers in the enterprise:

- Operational

- Tactical

- Strategic

The basic is shown in Figure 3-3.

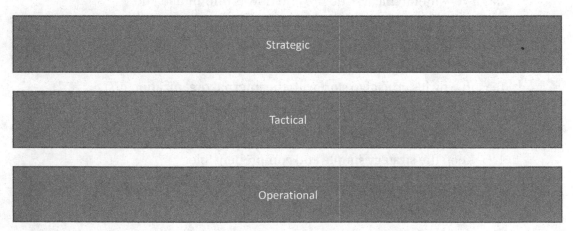

Figure 3-3. *Enterprise tiers*

Nothing new under the sun here, but what if we translate these tiers into something more practical? Think of the following:

- **Services (operational)**: At operational level the enterprise delivers the services and products. Typically, this is the customer-facing level, not only through delivery but also in support.

- **Contracts (tactical)**: To enable delivery and support, enterprises work through contracts. If we unbundle and rebundle the enterprise in smaller units or micro-enterprises that are closer to the customer, we need contracts – service-level agreements – between the unit and the customer to start with. What may a customer expect in terms of services?

  The micro-enterprises are part of ecosystems, as we will see. Hence, we need also contracts between the micro-enterprises, as we need APIs between microservices. We need agreements on performance indicators. In the traditional enterprise with separate business units, we would work with OLA, or operational-level agreements, and back-to-back agreements with suppliers of the enterprise. In the new enterprise, we work with ecosystem microcommunity contracts (EMC). We will explain this in the next section about integrating micro-enterprises with the transformation strategy.

  Just to clarify, this book is not a guide to implementing micro-enterprises. Micro-enterprises are a way to drive the transformation of large, more monolithic-based enterprises, making these enterprises more agile and enabling a greater customer intimacy. For an in-depth guide to micro-enterprises, we refer to, for instance, the site of Boundaryless.io that provides toolkits to implement this organizational model.

- **Enterprise governance (strategic)**: On strategic level we need governance. Someone needs to have the full overview to stay in control. This is the level where the strategy is set, with all policies, guidelines, and guardrails. This is also the place where EA is executed.

Our basic three-tier model is now enhanced (Figure 3-4).

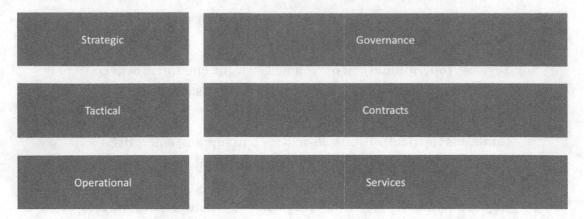

Figure 3-4. *Expanded enterprise tiers*

We are still working on our TOM. What are the steps to define the TOM, the desired state, or future mode of operations?

1. **Assessment**: The problem with this is that every consultancy firm will start with this and it always sounds like something obvious, time-consuming and thus costly. Yet, an assessment is a necessary step. But, we need to focus – focus on what capabilities the enterprise currently has and what capabilities are required.

2. **Strategic goal**: What does the enterprise want to achieve by implementing the future mode and the TOM?

3. **Tactical**: Who is part of the ecosystem and where does the enterprise needs to settle contracts or agreements? This also applies for the internal units. Remember that we will unbundle and rebundle the enterprise.

4. **Operational**: What are the key performance indicators (KPI) and how do services need to be arranged to fulfill these KPIs?

5. **Governance**: Part of the FMO is setting up the governance structure. There's one simple question that must be answered at the end of the day: who's responsible? But here lies a big risk: Enterprise tends to slip into a very complex governance structure, smothering the agility of the enterprise. Complex governance requires a lot of meetings that basically do not add to the delivery

of products and services. Keep it simple. This also means that trust
must become of the core values. Trust the micro-enterprises, for
instance.

The next question is, how we will organize this and how is this driving the desired
state after the transformation? The transformation should allow the enterprise to enter
the state of continuous innovation. What do we need for that from an EA point of view?
We can define five pillars for that in the transformation roadmap. These five pillars are
the basics of the order of digitization. You will surely recognize these by now, since they
overlap with the order that we discussed earlier.

- **Pillar 1**: Basic infrastructure

- **Pillar 2**: Applications and services

- **Pillar 3**: Innovation

- **Pillar 4**: Research and development

- **Pillar 5**: Human resources

These pillars can be plotted on our tiered enterprise model. By doing that, we're
creating an organizational matrix, as shown in Figure 3-5. It immediately shows that the
enterprise tiers of strategic, tactical, and operational are valid in every single pillar.

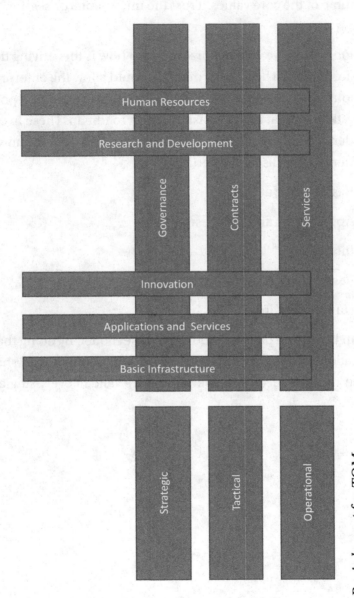

Figure 3-5. *Basic layout for TOM*

A more detailed TOM filled with all components could look like Figure 3-6. It shows that innovation needs to be covered on all layers.

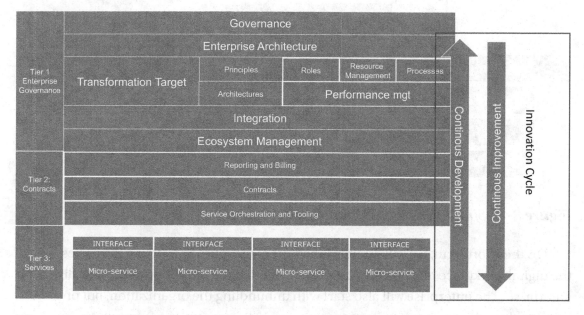

Figure 3-6.   *Detailed blueprint for TOM*

Innovation is not solely about technology, which is merely just an enabler of innovation. It's about people working together, creating new ideas. These people must come from all entities in an enterprise and preferable also customers. In the first two pillars, we have established a foundation to enable innovation. New ideas that seem viable enough enter the stage of research and development so that these ideas can be further developed into minimal viable products (MVPs) and tested.

For all of this, we need the right people with the right skills: that's why there's a fifth pillar for human resources. Together they form the new enterprise. But if we would try to transform the entire earth-born enterprise with this mindset, we are bound to fail. The golden rule "leverage the power of small" applies for everything. We must start small, with one or two teams. If we do that, we are already creating a blueprint for the micro-enterprise structure that we can later expand, as we will see further in this section.

Now we need to plan this on a timescale by defining a comprehensible roadmap, following our main stages: initiate, adopt, and expand. These stages can easily be translated into short, mid, and long term. It's shown in Figure 3-7.

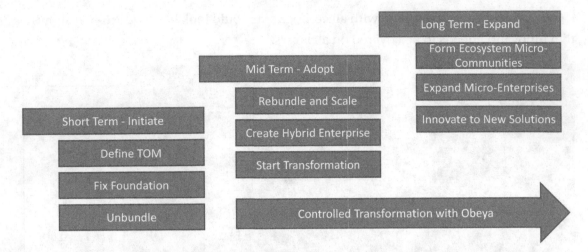

Figure 3-7. *Simplified transformation roadmap*

On the short term, we will establish the start of the journey by fixing the basics: the digital workplace, the infrastructure, and with that the backbone of the new digital enterprise. The enterprise will also start with unbundling the organization, but on a small scale with one or two units or teams.

Now we can start scaling and create a hybrid enterprise, the midterm plan. Unbundling and rebundling an enterprise are not activities that we do overnight. Here once more the golden rule of "leveraging the power of small" applies.

This is a good moment to take another look at these micro-enterprises and the role they can play in achieving this roadmap. Our goal is to have enterprises transform into smaller, more agile operating units that are close to the customer, where they can capture the Voice of the Customer. In general, this means that we have to unbundle the traditional enterprise. This is not something that hasn't been done before, on the contrary. Boundaryless offers open source adoption guide and toolkits to perform this unbundling and rebundling into micro-enterprises.

As said, a lot of big enterprises have already done this. Amazon and Spotify are examples. Indeed, these are cloud-born enterprises. Yet, the traditional earth-born enterprises can learn a great deal from these companies. They are organized in small self-managed teams that focus on specific services or products. At the same time, they are part of a larger organization that takes care of overarching business processes such as HR and, indeed, generic IT of which the workplace is likely the best example. And, they are part of ecosystems in which the teams collaborate with other companies and teams. Hence, the modern enterprise consists of micro-enterprises, facilitated by shared services platforms for HR and other generic processes and something that in Rendanheyi is called ecosystem microcommunity contract, next to the micro-enterprises and the shared services.

The Ecosystem Microcommunity Contract (EMC) is a sort of glue between different micro-enterprises, aiming for collaboration and co-creation. Rendanheyi distinguishes two types of these EMCs: the experience EMC and the solution EMC. The experience EMC is focusing on improving user experience, while the solution EMC provides services to micro-enterprises to help them create solutions in developing products and services.

Let's recap: on a short term we have deployed the basics of the TOM. In midterm the adoption has started, by creating the first micro-enterprises entering a hybrid mode. The final stage is the long-term ideation to the innovation enterprise, where the TOM is expanded and more digital services are adopted. Concepts such as data-driven and event-driven will be fully adopted, including a high degree of automation. We will discuss this in the next chapter, since these concepts must be integrated in and guided from architecture.

One important question hasn't been answered yet: How does the enterprise keep track of these changes? As part of this book, we provide a battle card that is based on the principles of Obeya. Obeya, Japanese for "big room," allows the enterprise to focus on the results while accelerating the transformation. The power of Obeya is that it visually brings together all available information that is relevant for the transformation: strategy, achievements, projects, improvements, and resources, next to the goals of the transformation. Bottlenecks – that we would prefer to call inhibition points, referring to Chapter 2 – are immediately visible, showing where mitigating actions to improve are required. Obeya is a perfect way to limit the number of formal meetings and just keep going, but in a controlled manner. A template for Obeya that can be used as the battle card is shown on the next page.

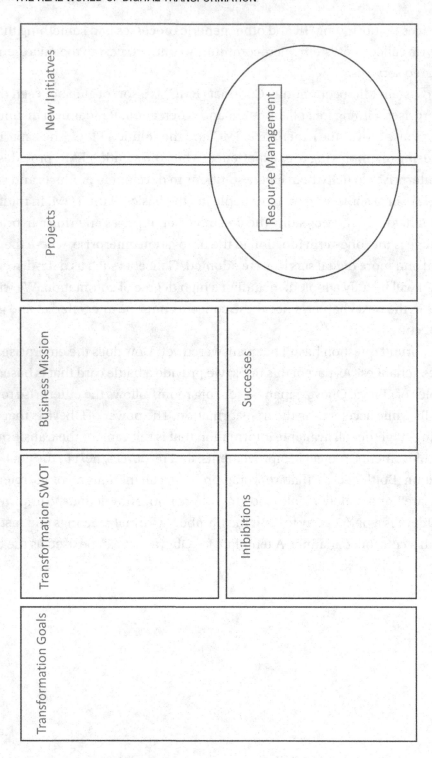

In the Obeya wall, the teams fill out the goals that they have and perform a SWOT analysis: strengths, weaknesses, opportunities, and threats. Weaknesses and threats might lead to inhibitions, but these are only listed when they materialize. Opportunities and strengths might result in new initiatives. Finished tasks are successes when realized within time and budget, but successes are also new initiatives that are rewarded and can be launched from the projects. Resource management is a vital process.

In Obeya the team doesn't only list how many people are working on projects, but also how the team is performing and "feeling." Staff that is not happy will not perform. More important, what is the cause of the feeling? Since it may and probably will lead to (new) inhibition points, it's important that staff is optimally facilitated to perform their job. Only then, new initiatives will be launched and goals achieved.

Application Portfolio Management

We have a TOM defined, a roadmap to reach that new state, and we have identified all the components that will be impacted by the transformation, including the well-being of staff. Basically, we have set up the backbone for our new, digitized enterprise. Good chance that we need to redesign our application portfolio as well, likely moving to SaaS and subscription models like we introduced SaaS to our workers with subscriptions for office applications. That's the model where we want to grow our own business.

Tien Tzuo, founder and CEO of "subscription evangelists" Zuora, states in his book *Subscribed* that subscription models will be the future of any company. In this book he predicts the end of ownership, which is pretty drastic. The problem he saw with "old" businesses was that they create a product, try to sell as many of the product as possible, and by doing that, dilute fixed costs and compete on margins. In Tien's view, that model is no longer sustainable. In his book he introduces some interesting concepts. One of them is staying in beta forever and, thus, keep innovating. There's the new enterprise. It continuously listens to customers and continuously innovates.

This is hard for a lot of enterprises: it's a complete paradigm shift. Tzuo mentions Google's Gmail as a perfect example of this paradigm shift. Gmail is never finished, as it none of Google's products – or any other SaaS for that matter. It's always in beta mode and is continuously updated and improved with new functionality including integrations with other services, even from other providers. Yet, Google did remove the word beta from the Gmail logo, since no company wants to rely on unfinished products. But, it's the future.

Continuously innovate thus means that a product is never finished. Consumers have got used to this in the meantime. The apps on their smartphones, tablets, and computers are continuously updated and upgraded – up until the point where a service or product reaches the end of its lifecycle. This is a good moment to explore the concept of lifecycles and especially lifecycle management a bit more.

Lifecycle and lifecycle management have become the most important aspects of applications and the underlying software. Perhaps it's more appropriate to say that lifecycle management is the one crucial process in the modern enterprise. Product lifecycle, information lifecycle, and application lifecycle are complementary. It encompasses almost everything that we discussed in the previous sections:

- Requirements

- Architecture

- Development

- Testing

- Deployment

- Continuous integration

- Operations

- Release management

From release management the cycle starts over again with requirements, since from the release onward, customers will formulate new demands and thus require new features to be developed. The cycle is maintained up until the point where a product, service, or application can't technically be updated and upgraded any longer, or – and this is more often the case – it simply takes too much effort and thus costs compared to developing a new product. Business planning, expected business outcomes, and the derived business case must always be leading in this process.

This has drastic implications for the architecture. The customers are subscribing to services that the enterprise provisions through digital channels. Customers order, upgrade, suspend, resume, and renew subscriptions. Thus, underlying services must be able to respond to this: scale up, down, suspend, provision (seamless) upgrades. To make it more complex, this needs to be able to any platform, at any time at any place.

This is all the domain of application management. Yet, every application must adhere to a number of quality attributes. We distinguish seven attributes to which every application must be validated:

1. **Interoperability**: The possibility for systems to interact with each other, based on standards, protocols, and policies.

2. **Configurability**: The ability to modify systems to a desired state.

3. **Performance**: The level on which a system functions according to specifications.

4. **Discoverability**: The easiness to find a system through, for instance, portals or browsers.

5. **Robustness**: The level of resilience of a system, for example, how fast does a system recover from failure?

6. **Portability**: The easiness to transfer a system to different platforms.

7. **Usability**: The easiness to use the system.

In the application portfolio, these are translated into architecture principles:

1. **Customer first**: This is by far the most important rule. Enterprises exist because they have customers. Hence, enterprise systems, also internal systems, must be designed, developed, and deployed with the customer in mind.

2. **Data-driven architecture**: The enterprise takes decisions based on data. This data will allow enterprises to serve their customers better.

3. **Event-driven architecture**: Systems respond to actions that are triggered by customer requests. This is an important principle in automation and especially in business models that are subscription-based. When a customer requests a subscription to a service, a number of activities are set in motion, making sure that the customer gets the services or products they're subscribed for.

4. **Test-driven architecture**: Test-driven development is another important principle in digital transformation. It allows enterprises

to speed up development dramatically since developers will not write extensive code or procedures to start with. In test-driven environments, an initial test scenario is executed showing the failures. These failures form the input to write and continuously improve code.

5. **Focus on the seven quality attributes**: In data-driven, event-driven, and test-driven, the seven quality attributes are leading at all times.

6. **Focus on change** – "leverage the power of small": Don't try to boil the ocean. Start with one project; learn and use the experience for the next projects. The same applies for the organization of the enterprise. Start with one unit, reform, transform, learn, and use the experience to transform the next units.

7. **Architect for microservices**: In a way this is also about "leveraging the power of small." Let teams work on one service. Microservices are easier to upgrade and update. But again, this only works when the quality attributes are taken into account, especially the ones about interoperability and discoverability. It requires teams to work together: as developers and operators and as teams with other teams.

8. **Architect for build, test, and deploy**: This may seem a bit obvious, but too often the architecture focuses on the end state of a service or a product. Architecture also describes how to get from A to B. A solution is not just the desired state, but how to get to the desired state. That's the transformation.

9. **Adopt shift-left**: This is about shifting responsibility. EA will provide guardrails and guidelines, while teams will be responsible for development, test, and deployment of services and products. Shift-left is a crucial element in adopting micro-enterprises. These must be allowed to operate quite autonomously and take decisions, based on requirements that they receive from customers. That is true shift-left: moving processes and resources closer to the customer, enabling faster solutions that satisfy the customer needs.

10. **Zero trust**: Security must be integrated, it's not something "on top off." It means that enterprises have to take security measures throughout every single artifact in the architecture. Security is intrinsic. Basic rule: Never trust, always verify. It applies to persons, but to systems too. In digital everything is an identity. Treat systems as such. In Chapter 4, we will look further into security.

To enable this, we build scalable, agile platforms. Indeed, here's where digital really comes in with concepts such as cloud native, DevOps, everything as code, and everything as a service. We'll explore these concepts in more detail before we start defining our new enterprise portfolio.

- **Cloud native**: The term cloud native is typically used with applications. Cloud-native apps are apps that are loosely linked to the underlying infrastructure needed to support them. Today, that means deploying microservices through containers that can be dynamically provisioned with resources based on user demand. Each microservice can communicate independently through APIs. Microservices provide the advantages of modularity, portability, and granular control over resources.

- **DevOps and DevSecOps**: Literally, this means that developers and operators work together in one team, where in the more traditional way of working developers would work independently from the operators. The philosophy behind DevOps is that development and deployment can be more efficient and faster when developers and operators work together. Since DevOps teams work with code and application pipelines, security must be integrated from the start of development to deployment into production. In other words, security is not added when the application is ready to go into production. Integrating security in DevOps is referred to as DevSecOps.

- **Everything as code**: Not only applications are built with code, resources running that application are also defined by code. Compute nodes, networks, and storage are all captured in code when applications are deployed in cloud. The benefit of this is that the infrastructure hosting the applications can be integrated in the DevOps/DevSecOps pipelines, merging the application code with the code defining the running platform.

- **Anything as a service**: The best-known example of the concept anything as a service is subscriptions. Consumers don't buy products or services, but submit subscriptions that they can stop, suspend, restart, and modify. This can be done with everything: hardware as a service (HaaS), database as a service (DbaaS), communications as a service (CaaS). All this technology serves other even more physical services, such as package delivery to homes or healthcare services such as remote patient monitoring.

We can now define our new landscape. It might start to look something like the concept shown in Figure 3-8.

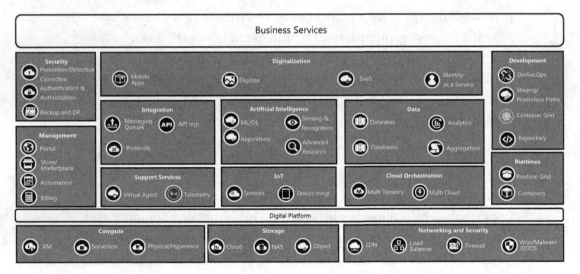

Figure 3-8. *Example of digital platform architecture (used and adapted by courtesy of Pascal Huijbers)*

The new digital application portfolio must reflect the strategy of the transformed enterprise. The golden rules for this are

- **Flexibility**
  - Ease of use for developers
  - Developing platform agnostic through microservices and containers, using native technology

- **Agility**
  - Capture requirements of businesses faster, using QFD, HOQ, and VOC
  - Development and deployment against standards and guardrails
  - Continuous improvement through short iterations by seamless integration between apps, containers, container, orchestration
  - Onboarding process through API orchestration
  - Single-pane glass observability
  - Automation and shift-left leading to less effort in operations; shift focus to development and innovation
  - Use existing platforms and market places
- **Speed**
  - Use industry standards off the shelf
  - Adopt open source mentality across all businesses
  - Adopt test-driven development

In Chapter 4, you will learn how enterprises can adopt agile processes, start working successfully with Dev(Sec)Ops, and integrate it all in "floating architecture" – since the architecture in a modern, digital enterprise is never fixed nor finished. Enterprise architects will constantly have to adopt changes and integrate them in the EA. That sounds risky, and frankly, it is. The last section of this chapter is therefor about risks and controlling risks.

Controlling Risks

Any change comes with risks. In fact, implementing a new EA comes with significant risks. As a result of changing EA, processes, products, and services will change in the enterprise. The new EA will trigger new designs and redesigns. That will inevitably introduce risks. If the enterprise adopts agile working and DevOps, it inherently accepts the chance on failures. We already mentioned test-driven development (TDD) in which a test is conducted, and based on the failures in the test, applications are developed.

Developers will only start developing when the test has failed. Failure is an accepted artifact in the modern, digital enterprise.

That doesn't mean that risks associated with failures are accepted. In Chapter 4, we will extensively explain how agile and DevOps must be set up to avoid failures and associated risks to materialize in production environments. So, we still need to be aware of risks and be ready to counter these.

To calculate risks, failure mode and effect analysis (FMEA) is a good and very comprehensible methodology. It works with basically three parameters: severity, occurrence, and detection. What are the odds that a risk occurs, what is the severity when the risk materializes, and how fast can we detect the risk? Next, in FMEA enterprises must define actions to mitigate risks. Obviously, it depends on the priority of the risks to what level actions have to be taken and what is acceptable as residual risk after an action has been executed.

When do we need to execute FMEA? As part of the QFD. Let's have one more look at QFD. The process of QFD is used to capture and prioritize the needs of the customer. Using the House of Quality (HOQ), QFD helps us to focus on the most important aspects of the product or service. In that process, inconsistencies between requirements, the needs of the customer (remember the Voice of the Customer), and the risks are identified. For reference the HOQ matrix is shown in Figure 3-9.

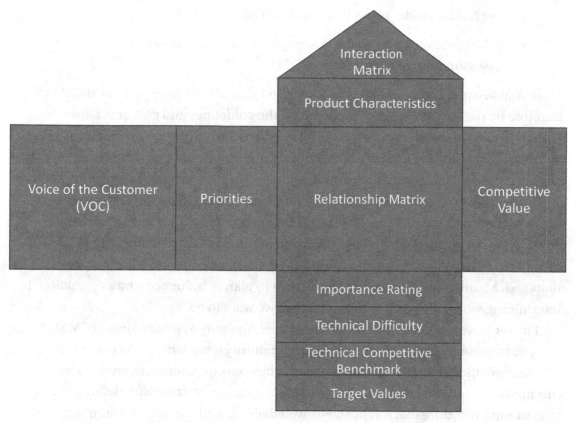

Figure 3-9. *House of quality matrix*

Risks will be identified by matching the requirements to technical difficulties and the analysis to competitive values – what is the position in relation to competition?

As a minimum, risk management procedures must cover:

- Scope of the product or service, taking the needs and expectations of customers into consideration. Does the product or service do or deliver what it's supposed to do or deliver?

- From the first question, the functions are derived. Assess per function in what way the function might fail. This is the failure mode in FMEA.

- Assess what the consequences are of the specific function failure. Consequences can occur in systems, related systems, but also for customers.

- How serious is the failure and how severe are the consequences?

- Per failure mode, assess what could possibly cause the failure.

- Take the results back to the design phase – remember that risk assessment is an integral part of QFD.

Risk assessment using FMEA is an integrated part of the whole process and should therefore be part of the EA. After all, in the EA the guidelines and guardrails are defined to execute the design processes for products and services. The modern, digital enterprise transforming itself to a continuously innovating company must address risk management and integrate it in the innovation process. It's part of the transformation.

Proper risk management requires a mature enterprise. Controlling risks therefore is intertwined with the maturity level of the enterprise. Hence, we must start with defining that maturity level. An enterprise that has implemented some form of EA doesn't necessarily have to be mature. Maturity has to do with how the enterprise is managed. Maturity models are one instrument to plan or influence a transformation, by determining where we stand today and where we want to go.

The most well-known maturity model is the Capability Maturity Model (CMM). Every enterprise wants to achieve the highest maturity level, where processes are well defined and controlled and moreover the business outcomes are predictable. This applies to all processes, including risk management, starting with defining a risk assessment procedure that is repeatable, well defined, and controlled. Ultimately, also risk management must lead predictable outcomes as risks can be identified, quantified, and mitigated from strategy, governed through EA.

Only by complying with risk management, organizations will be able to create and work in a coherent ecosystem, if consistently deployed across the micro-enterprises.

This forms the enterprise business backbone. In the next chapter we will further detail the digital architecture and learn how to integrate DevOps in our EA. Plus: We really need to start talking about security.

Summary

This was an important chapter. Before an enterprise can start with a digital transformation, it needs to define a new target operating model (TOM) enabling the enterprise to adopt digital services and use these to innovate its own portfolio. This is not just a matter of technology: the organization must be ready for it. By first transforming the backbone of the enterprise and adopting digital services, the company can set the strategy for the future mode of operations (FMO). This FMO will likely involve the adoption of new business models, such as subscriptions. This model implies that services must be architected around the customer. Modern enterprises must organize themselves in such way that it can quickly capture the needs of the customer, integrating these in the architectures of services and products. A basic roadmap was discussed, including a comprehensive methodology to track progress using Obeya.

The modern, digital enterprise will need agile, flexible platforms to continuously innovate its portfolio. The TOM must reflect this. The organization is unbundled in small, customer-focused units called micro-enterprises and new architecture principles are introduced, including data-driven, event-driven, and test-driven development. The result is a first, basic architecture for an enterprise landing on a digital platform, enabling innovation by using cloud-native services.

These are impactful changes to any organization. Changes come with risks. The final section of the chapter discusses risk management.

CHAPTER 4

Creating the Floating Architecture

Creating modern architecture patterns and trying to avoid the pitfalls of antipatterns, by adopting and applying the principles of DevOps. It will be a floating, dynamic architecture, but we will also learn how to stay in control through change management. Ultimately, we are creating architecture that enables business agility. That starts with culture and the right mindset.

Creating Continuous Architecture

The term continuous architecture was first launched by Murat Erder and Piere Pureur who wrote their book on the subject in 2015. The subtitle of that book was *Sustainable Architecture in an Agile and Cloud-Centric World* and that covered it very well. They define six principles to a modern architecture and, no surprise, these principles were largely discussed already in the previous section. The principles are focused around the quality attributes. Yet, in this section a few principles will be explored in a bit more detail since they form the foundation of the modern, agile architecture.

The key word is continuous. DevOps and agile are built on the principles of continuous with pipelines that enable continuous integration and continuous deployment. Why is that so important for modern enterprises and why should enterprise architects bother? Because it's crucial for the business of a digital enhance enterprise. The architecture must reflect agile. Relevant questions the enterprise architect should ask are as follows:

- Who are my customers?

- Are the products that the enterprise delivers fulfilling the needs of the customers?

© Jeroen Mulder 2023
J. Mulder, *Modern Enterprise Architecture*, https://doi.org/10.1007/978-1-4842-9066-8_4

- How does the enterprise measure customer satisfaction with the products?

- How does the enterprise measure customer satisfaction with the enterprise itself and especially the interaction with the enterprise?

- How much time does it take to include new features into existing products?

- How much time does it take to develop a new product?

- Are teams empowered to gather feedback from customers directly to improve products?

- Are teams empowered to change requirements based on that feedback in an autonomous way?

- Are the enterprise mission and goals crystal clear to the teams?

- Are teams empowered to structure themselves to be able to deliver the product at the highest quality?

- Are all of the preceding questions laid out in a clear enterprise structure with corresponding processes?

- Is the enterprise really adopting and embracing agile, working in true DevOps and with teams that are close to the customer?

Continuous architecture addresses these questions mainly in three principles:

- **Delay design decisions until they are necessary**: This is important in terms of responsiveness and acting when events occur, enabling to respond to changes.

- **Architect for change, or better continuous change**: But don't try to do everything at once, leverage the power of small, the topic of the next section.

- **Architect for build, test, and deploy, what we do in DevOps**: We will extensively discuss DevOps and DevSecOps in this chapter.

The risk of doing architecture is that we are only focusing on the technical side of it. The risk of doing that is that we are still creating big, static, almost monolithic architectures that "fix" the entire enterprise. Then we are creating boundaries, literally an enterprise cage. Instead, we want to create a floating architecture allowing the enterprise to move freely, adaptive, and agile. The continuous architecture framework addresses this.

That framework contains a way of working and a toolbox but includes two topics that are equally if not more important than architecture itself: roles and rituals, both forming the culture of an organization. In the final chapter of this book, we will address the role of the architect, but we can already say that this role is heavily changing. As we will learn that the architecture itself is not fixed and rigid anymore, so is the role of the architect. In agile teams, all members will have some architectural tasks. The enterprise architect, or lead architect as the person sometimes is referred to, will become more and more the servant leader. The continuous architecture framework still recognizes the enterprise architect though, as the person connecting the dots between business, data, and technology, but also as the coach overseeing all assets. Using reference models and patterns, the enterprise architect guides the teams in designing and building solutions in an "evolutionary" way.

Then we have rituals, meant to create and sustain a culture of collaboration between teams and all other stakeholders in the business. The continuous architecture framework identifies the dialog zone where teams can debate architecture and exchange ideas. This is analog to the ceremonies that teams have in agile working with daily scrums and sprint plannings. They all serve the same purpose: becoming agile.

Becoming Agile by Starting Small

It's an item that we addressed earlier in this book: If it's so important to start the digital transformation, why hasn't every company embraced it yet? The simple explanation for that is that most companies try to boil the ocean. A lot of projects that are started as part of the transformation never make it further than a pilot or proof of concept. Technology has got nothing to do with it. The inhibition for fulfilling a successful transformation lies in culture, resulting in a lacking strategic vision and the corresponding organization.

First of all, enterprises and enterprise architects need to realize one thing: not everyone in the enterprise will be convinced of the necessity of transformation. The middle mud is a famous entity in every organization. The middle mud is the layer that sits right under the top management where the strategy is unfolded. However, innovations rarely start at top management or C level. Typically, it starts in the layer where the actual work is done. Hence, it's important to start doing the Gemba walks. Here's where innovations gain ground.

That middle layer is not getting paid for being innovative, they are getting paid for keeping the lights on. This is typically the operations layer: innovations disrupt stable operations and therefore ops are usually not very promotive when it comes to innovation. That's how they run a stable business. Before innovations get to the decision-makers, they must also convince that middle layer. These managers must be involved from the very start. It's lesson number one in change and transformation: involve all stakeholders. In the section about change management, you will learn more about stakeholders and how to get them on board.

Lesson two is address the culture. It's crucial to engage change. Management of change is crucial to business agility, and with that, we're at the core of digital transformation: business agility.

Business agility is about adopting continuous change and making this a routine in the enterprise. Only an agile business will be able to respond and react to changing business demands, and even get ahead of the game by recognizing the change and start innovating its business to be prepared for emerging opportunities. In the previous chapter, the organization in micro-enterprises, adhering to the principles of Rendanheyi, has been extensively discussed. Business agility requires a nonhierarchical organization. Teams need to be close to the markets and the customers in that market, continuously interacting with customers. The insights that are gathered in these teams are fed back into the overarching mission and strategy of the enterprise. It's important that teams have a common understanding of the mission and the goals of the enterprise and how requirements are captured.

In the first place, this means that organizations themselves must become agile. A lot of organizations are still hierarchical organized. That's a traditional, top-down management style that is an inhibition to innovation. Innovation has become more important than ever. People must be enabled to work in network type of organizations where the place where they sit in the organization doesn't matter, but what they do for the company. People should be able to "float" through the network ecosystem of the enterprise, in pursuit of the best solution – wherever that solution is coming from. This is all culture.

The problem with this change is that outcomes might be lesser predictable and that's what's really scary in organizations, especially management. The effect of unpredictable outcomes is not the result of the changing organization, but simply because markets have become lesser predictable. Enterprises merely need to be ready to anticipate that unpredictive behavior of markets with rapidly changing demands and needs of customers.

Outcomes of projects are not easy to define in today's markets, but it's still the way enterprises run most of their projects – with predefined outcomes and an extensive planning. Changes to demands are hard to manage in this kind of project. Agile working allows organizations to adjust the outcome, typically the product, to changing demands and also align the planning to this change. This can only be done when projects are not managed as big, complex projects with a linear planning, but as a collective of smaller components. It's a complete change of mindset and it's an illusion to think that an enterprise can change this mindset overnight. This is part of the transformation and probably the part where the rule of "leveraging the power of small" applies best.

Take the monolithic application as an example. It's almost impossible to implement a change to a monolithic application without changing the whole application. The consequence will likely be that the entire application must be taken offline, upgraded, and tested as whole before it can be brought back online again. This is an utterly complex activity that requires a very detailed planning that must be followed. A change to a component will impact the entire planning – and the outcome.

Agile methods unfold this complexity by working in teams that concentrate on specific tasks. To get this to work, it's essential that there is a common understanding of mission, goals, and processes. All teams must have a common understanding of the greater project goals, project components, interactions between components and requirements. Yet, a team concentrates on a subset of tasks, enabling them to develop and deliver much faster. Key decisions are taken collaboratively, but teams have great autonomy in fulfilling their specific tasks.

Chapter 5 will be all about scaling the business and the enterprise, but here we will already discuss a methodology that helps in scaling through continuous iteration: DevOps.

DevOps is a method to speed up development and deployment. DevOps teams are smaller teams, yet with all disciplines represented: developers, testers, security professionals, and operators. They have been assigned with tasks and usually work in sprints of two to three weeks. The output of the task is integrated in the main product. In the section about the DevSecOps, these principles will be discussed in more detail. In DevSecOps, indeed, since security is always "on." We will learn about that too in this chapter.

First, let's have a better understanding of business agility and what the role of enterprise architecture should be in achieving business agility.

Definition and Purpose of Business Agility

Digital transformation helps to make enterprises business agile. But what is business agility? In a word, it's about making the enterprise adaptive. In the previous chapters we talked about inhibition: enterprises face a lot of inhibition in transforming business and the enterprise itself. Typically, the earth-born enterprise has a legacy, and legacy comes with debts. Debts – technical debt being one of them, but not exclusively – will slow down any change. You need to get rid of the debt to start with.

One of the biggest debts in creating an adaptive organization is the fact that an enterprise has no means to respond swiftly to changes and allocate resources to address the change. That's what business agility means: sense upcoming changes in an early stage, being able to respond fast to changes and to allocate resources to handle the change. To many companies this sounds very risky. Why? Because the agile company must have resources to do so: uncommitted resources. Most companies will label uncommitted resources as cost. We will talk about culture in a bit, but this is already a paradigm shift.

There's only one way to afford uncommitted resources, through automation, so that people can focus on creating value instead of fixing operational issues. It also requires standardization, but a completely standardized environment will not provide the necessary flexibility. It's a balance that an enterprise must find.

In short,

- Business agility enables business to reactive swiftly to changes, not constraint by static, rigid architecture, and forthcoming designs.

- Business agility offers business the capabilities to deal with unexpected events that influence or impact the business.

The purpose of business agility is

- To stimulate and enable innovation

- To improve the value propositions while

- Reducing risks

Business agility is achieved by

- Providing options. In the end, that's what architecture is about: options.

- Observability of changes

- Freedom to navigate

- Creating the capability of taking swift, immediate action through Faster responsiveness

- Increasing predictability through increased insights

- Reiterating business processes fast in response to customers' needs, through capturing the Voice of the Customer

- Establishing the capability to allocate resources quickly and faster than competitors

- The ability and the courage to change collaborations in the enterprise ecosystem

EA principles to enhance business agility are

- Remove constraints, get rid of silos

- Taking the customer-first principle and closely following the customer's journey

- Realize that it's about experience that matters to customers, more than the product itself

- Lean management

- Collecting and managing portfolio

- Collecting and managing initiatives for innovations

- Model and manage agile processes

- Automate where it makes sense

- Embrace the data-driven principles in architecture

- Enable fast decision-making

- Communicate, communicate, communicate

This is crucial to start the change. That change is vital to the business agility. Business agility must be guided through architecture, including agile working and DevSecOps. But first we need to address one other question: Why does an enterprise need to become business agile? The answer: To survive disruption and start leading by innovation.

Beat Disruption, Lead by Innovation

Disruption is a buzzword. On the other hand, it's something that is real and will impact a lot of businesses. Almost every business on this planet must get itself ready to respond to fast-changing markets and client behavior. This in itself triggers continuous change, potential risk for the stability of systems. Enterprises need methodologies and systems that are able

- To create uncommitted resources in an enterprise that can respond to change when required.

- This means that enterprises have to automate the common and the respective operations. In Site Reliability Engineering (SRE), this is referred to as "toil," and enterprises must find ways to eliminate toil in order to have people freed up to work on new demands.

- This implicates those automated systems must be able to predict business impact when something in the entire supply and delivery chain fails.

- Systems are able to mitigate the expected impact before the event occurs.

All of this must be extremely scalable. Chapter 5 will be all about scalability.

But especially earth-born (traditional) enterprises face a lot of challenges in turning themselves around. They must disrupt themselves before they can start to beat the disruption and become leaders. Inhibition points are as follows:

- Disconnect between business and IT. IT is often more advanced and ready to start adopting new technology but fails to convince the business of the added value.

- Enterprises implement agile frameworks, start small, but next, fail to scale.

- The migration and transformation to cloud turns out to be more complex than expected.

- Last, but not least, the war on talent. Professionals are getting scarce since competition is fierce.

How can enterprises overcome these inhibitions?

1. Business and IT must develop a joint ambition and strategy. This is the North Star.

2. The target operating model must focus on eliminating toil by automation to create uncommitted resources.

3. The enterprise must be unbundled and rebundled in teams that are close to the costumer, capturing the voice of the customer, and focus on the work in value streams to create the desired value for that customer. Obviously, this must be in line with the North Star, the joint ambition.

This can only be achieved through enterprise disruption. The EA will have the task to advice and help create the long-term vision that supports the ambition. There has to be guidance in the direction wherein the enterprise has to move. The North Star is setting the destination, but it doesn't tell you how to reach that destination. The power of the North Star is that it's simple. We will get to speak about antipatterns later on, but on the main antipatterns in modern architecture are that architectures try to capture everything and become way too detailed. It will make the architecture incomprehensible and, worse, not agile and not actionable.

From the North Star, the unbundled teams must get the opportunity and the room to iterate toward that joint ambition. Remember, transformation is about humans in the first place. There must be sense of urgency and willingness throughout the entire enterprise to adopt the change. Digital transformation is a human transformation.

In summary, the EA of the modern enterprise must enable

- Strategic planning

- Functional transformation to support the ambition and the strategy through iterative steps

- Resource allocation, making sure that resources are available to respond to changing markets and customer behavior

Of course, technology plays an important role. It's the driver for innovation, but only if it's fully integrated into the business. Technology for the sake of technology is worthless. Innovation is the lifeline of the modern enterprise. The innovation process is characterized by four stages:

- Challenge

- Focus

- Develop

- Validate

You have recognized this by now: innovation is an iterative process and must be embedded in the overall ambition and derived strategy of the enterprise. It's another reason why enterprise architects must refrain from being too detailed and creating the architecture ivory tower, a term introduced by tech leader and blogger Jo Crossick (refer to https://medium.com/@jocrossick/using-a-north-star-to-guide-emergent-architecture-a0941c0c5177). We don't need the ivory tower, but we need a floating architecture. Something that floats has little friction, but just enough friction in order not to sink – a floating object just has enough mass to float, free to move in every direction and gain speed.

Enterprise architects "are like sailors who have to rebuild their ship on the open sea, without ever being able to dismantle it in dry dock and reconstruct it from the best components." This analogy is called Neurath's boat, after the Austrian philosopher Otto Neurath. It's absolutely true for the modern EA.

Security Is Intrinsic

So far, we haven't been discussing about security a lot. We discussed setting up a new structure for the enterprise and implementing a new, agile way of working, empowered and enabled by that new structure. We talked about starting the transformation of the enterprise and how the various layers of the enterprise are impacted by the need for digital transformation. There's an undeniable need for that transformation, since customers are changing their behavior in how they purchase and use products and services. Their demands and thus requirements are changing almost on a daily basis, calling for continuous – or floating – architecture that is as elastic as the customer.

There's one more thing that is even more challenging than the changing demands of customers: the threats that digitally enabled enterprise face. Products and services are enabled to be consumed at any time, at any place, on a variety of devices. With big data, artificial intelligence, and Internet of things, enterprises and their customers are connected almost 7/24 where AI engines analyze behavior using a continuous stream of data. Data is shared across a multitude of platforms; systems interact continuously with other systems. Yet, security is still not top of mind in every enterprise. The phrase "top of mind" has been chosen deliberately, since security management is a matter of mindset. It all starts with security hygiene.

What is security hygiene? For starters, enforcing people to have complex passwords that are renewed regularly – better, have systems doing it for them, using biometric options such as fingerprint, palm vein, or face recognition – but also not opening suspicious emails. Or this, filling in game questions such as "What was the name of your first dog" on social media platforms. It's a phishing trick.

Next, enterprises need to do everything they can to protect their systems and their customers. This must be a default. Too often enterprises have a sort of pick-and-choose strategy when it comes to security – implementing processes and tools to keep passwords secure and installing firewalls to protect networks, but not executing daily backups or performing disaster recovery tests. The reason for this pick-and-choose strategy is costs.

Security is not a menu, something you can choose from. It's intrinsic in everything the enterprise does. The EA must integrate security on every single layer of the EA. This includes

- Documented security policies and procedures that are regularly updated

- System hardening and other security parameters to protect environments from threats

- Proactive vulnerability management

- Lifecycle management including patching, updates, and upgrades

- Testing procedures and processes

- Automation

From this point onward, we will not talk about DevOps anymore, but about DevSecOps. Security policies are applied from the first moment a development starts, up until the product or service is used by the customer. The enterprise must mature in this area, and this is not an easy task. The DevSecOps Maturity Model (DSOMM) shown in Figure 4-1 can be of great help in guiding the enterprise and integrating DevSecOps in the EA.

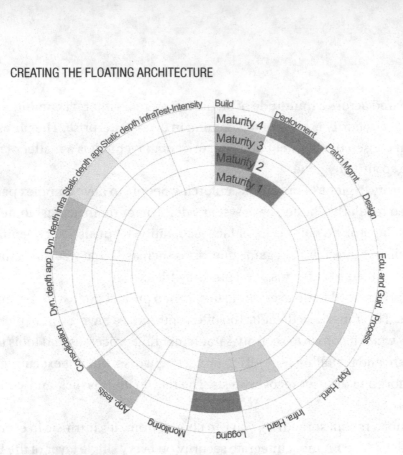

Figure 4-1. *The DevSecOps Maturity Model by OWASP*

DSOMM shows all aspects an enterprise should fulfill in terms of security in DevOps, including

- Design

- Patch management

- Infrastructure hardening

- Application hardening

- Logging

- Monitoring

- Testing

- Education and guidance

- Processes

Using the DSOMM will help identify the current position of the enterprise in terms of security and also help in setting the ambition by implementing DevSecOps. It's the topic of the next section.

Including DevSecOps Principles

First, why is DevOps relevant to modern companies? Microsoft CEO Satya Nadella explained it very well in his keynote for Microsoft Inspire 2022: "Today every company is a digital company. In fact, there's more demand for developers in some key industries, like public sector, education, energy, retail, entertainment and transportation, than even the tech industry itself. This represents a tremendous opportunity for all of you. Organizations are eager to equip fusion teams of pro and citizen developers with best-in-class tooling so that they can scale their impact together. And they are eager to adopt DevOps, which is fast becoming the default way to deploy code to production, creating massive opportunity for all of you to help them adopt these new processes."

Next question, why do we need DevSecOps? Take a house, for example. A burglary is a matter of minutes. At least, so it seems. In practice, a burglar often keeps an eye on targets for some time in advance. The burglar will usually first explore where the weak points are in, for example, hinges and locks. They may keep an eye on the house and its inhabitants for a while to know when the house has been vacated. They base their plan on that. In other words, a criminal often watches certain behavior for much longer and has already studied objects well so that they know where the vulnerabilities – the weak spots – are.

We see the same behavior in cybercriminals: explore, plan, strike. Without this awareness, every model and every tool don't stand a chance in protecting assets.

Ask any CIO, CDO, or IT manager about the biggest challenge in the field and the answer will most likely be security. That makes sense. Threats and attacks on organizations' IT environments are becoming more numerous and, above all, more resourceful. It is precisely this creativity in inventing new ways to compromise systems that is worrying – not to mention the speed with which criminals display this creativity. Many an organization would pay a fortune if they could develop the same speed in inventing and developing new products and services.

Organizations are trying to do that: to match that speed when it comes to development. That's where agile and DevOps come in, including automation. In practice, organizations suddenly make security a neglected child in this entire process of

DevOps and automation. Security checks are only performed once the application has been technically tested and approved. Often those checks do not extend beyond static checks of code. The latter is called SAST in technical terms: static application security testing. A SAST tool scans application source code and its components to identify potential vulnerabilities. Problem: In practice, these tools capture about fifty percent of existing vulnerabilities.

In addition to SAST, we also have DAST: dynamic application security testing. DAST tools actively scan for vulnerabilities in web applications using penetration testing. Issue: These scans are time-consuming, and the exact location of a vulnerability is (usually) not found. So, are these scans enough? The answer is simple: no.

To get an idea of a thorough DevSecOps implementation, it is best to look at OWASP's DevSecOps Maturity Model (DSOMM). Most organizations will achieve the first level of this model, although level 1 already requires far-reaching measures such as application hardening, isolated infrastructure, and encryption at various levels. Level 4 should be the ultimate goal of every organization involved in DevOps – on the way to DevSecOps. At this level, we talk about applying blue/green deployment, chaos monkey, and in-depth testing.

With blue/green deployment, two separate, but identical environments are created: one environment (blue) for existing functionality in production and one environment (green) for new applications, completely separated from production. Chaos monkey is a technique in which virtual machines or containers are randomly switched off or even removed to see what the impact is on a production environment. It's one of many tests being conducted in DevSecOps to see what happens when environments are attacked by hackers. By taking measures such as these to a higher level, security as an integral part of the development and management process, it remains possible to stay ahead of criminals. After all, we all want to be safe in our home or office!

Do we have to do all this? Short and sweet: yes. But the most important thing is and remains awareness. The realization that criminals can and will take a look very early on if you do not have your security in order throughout the entire development chain. Like the burglar drives through the streets late at night to see when people are at home or not.

Now, let's have a closer look at the requirements of DevSecOps. Before we do that, we're listing all the activities that are included in the DevOps cycle (Figure 4-2). All these activities must be embedded and supported from the EA. These activities form the operational layer of our overarching model that will be presented in the section about the architecture vision.

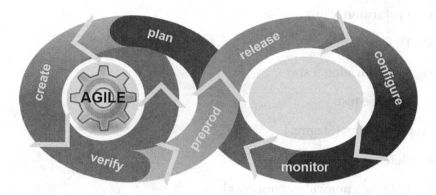

Figure 4-2. *The DevOps cycle*

The following activities must be included per stage:

1. Plan

    • Production metrics

    • Requirements definition (use case, prototyping)

    • Business metrics (performance, resolution times, customer satisfaction)

    • New feature/function priorities and fixes

    • Release plan (timing, business case)

    • Security policy, adherence, and requirements

2. Develop

    • Design (software, configuration)

    • Code, code merge, code quality, and performance

    • Functional test

    • Release candidate

3. Test (Verify)

    • Acceptance test

    • Regression test

    • Static analysis (quality and compliance)

    • Security analysis (vulnerability)

- Performance test
- Defect status
- Configuration test
- Release test

4. Preproduction (Staging)

- Release staging/holding
- Release approval/preapproval

5. Release

- Scheduled/timed release
- Release coordination
- Deploy application
- Deployment status
- Change controls
- Fallback/recovery

6. Configure

- Infrastructure provisioning and configuration
- Application provisioning and configuration

7. Monitor

- Performance and availability of the IT infrastructure, network, and application
- End-user response and experience

From monitor the feedback loops back into plan.

How does security merge into this? DevSecOps is implemented in three "layers," starting with education since security is first and foremost about awareness in the teams. Teams will have to learn that every choice they make in development and deployment comes with a consequence. That applies to costs, but even more so to security. In the end, this has to do with awareness and culture in the enterprise. Why? Because it also requires a high amount of trust of the teams.

We can define the implementation in three phases:

- **Phase 1: Education and training**

  This starts with a proper assessment.

  - Documenting the current state of any processes

  - Gathering any reporting data about your current development processes

  - Identifying what's working and not working in your development processes by interviewing key developers

  Since no organization can buy DevSecOps, the enterprise needs to implement and foster a DevSecOps culture that is characterized by

  - Continuous feedback

  - Container-based and microservices architecture

  - Team autonomy

  - Training

- **Phase 2: Integrate security in DevOps cycles**

  In this phase we integrate security processes and tools into the DevOps lifecycle. This phase integrates security tools into these existing DevOps toolchains. This phase is also the time to perform a security audit on continuous integration and continuous delivery/ deployment (CI/CD) toolchains to ensure security.

- **Phase 3: Introduce or enhance automation**

  Businesses need to create an automation roadmap that charts how they will introduce automation into their respective toolchains. Start small ("leverage the power of small") and expand with automation across the various toolchains. Seek a small project such as a patch or a feature update to test the implementation plan.

Automate one build, quality assurance, or security check for one of the DevOps teams as a proof-of-concept project. Document the findings from this small project, especially the lessons learned and any other feedback from the DevOps team members working on the project.

Hopefully it's clear why organizations should not just implement DevOps, but include security in the DevOps cycle. The one reason why organizations don't do this is this misperception: security is slowing us down. That's true – if you don't integrate security with the other agile processes. Usually, the handover between dev and ops then stops at something that is called a firewall. Application code is tested, and all is fine. Then it needs to be deployed, but then security kicks in. What firewall ports need to be opened? Those need to be listed and requested through a rigid security process. Your two-week sprint is gone by then.

DevSecOps reveals the friction and the pain points between development, security, and the business. DevSecOps is also the road to remove these pain points. For starters, organizations that start implementing DevSecOps will inevitably face issues that will slow down the agile processes. That's a phase where organizations will have to go through in order to identify the pain points and find out ways to remove them, by defining processes, getting tools in place, and ultimately automating the process.

Revealing friction and finding ways to solve these require change. And where's change, there's change management – the topic of the next section.

Change Management in Floating Architecture

Change management and continuous improvement are not the same, but they are necessary in every modern enterprise. The principles of change management do apply to continuous improvement as well. Both need

- Sponsorship
- Impact assessment
- Readiness assessment
- Mitigation plan

A common methodology to rate changes is through the plan–do–check–act cycle (PDCA). Changes are planned, implemented, and evaluated, leading to adjustments and improvements in coming changes. In summary,

- **Plan**: Look at current work and design a plan for improving this work. Set objectives for this improvement.

- **Do**: Carry out the planned improvement in a controlled trial setup.

- **Check**: Measure the result of the improvement and compare it with the original situation and check it against the set objectives.

- **Act**: Adjust based on the results found at check.

This works fine as a process, but it doesn't say anything about the quality of the changes itself. The issue with this PDCA cycle is that it doesn't take into account that during the cycle, conditions might change. They will change, requiring calibration all the time. This is a good point to have a proper look at the definitions of change management and continuous improvement.

We need something else than PDCA. Luckily, an alternative exists. It's called OODA which stands for observe, orient, decide, and act. OODA is a perfect process to manage continuous changes. It was originally invented by a US Air Force fighter pilot, John Boyd. The power of the OODA loop lies in the second O: orientation. Orientation is influenced by cultural heritage and experiences, among others. Next, orientation influences the way we observe events. The method was developed to rapidly respond to movements of hostile fighter aircraft, but later it was adopted by business too.

Decision-makers in business observe behavior of customers, but this is filtered through predictions of behavior by competitors. This filtering is orientation, and it influences the decisions of the business. The more accurate the orientation is and information can be applied to the orientation, the better and faster decisions can be taken, resulting in business, competitive advantages. The goal of OODA is to "get inside" the thinking of the competition and use that in the decision-making. If we can do that, we can respond to changes fast and even be ahead of them and prepare the enterprise for upcoming events. The OODA loop is shown in Figure 4-3.

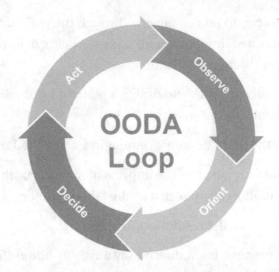

Figure 4-3. *The OODA loop*

Let's explore the four stages of the OODA loop in a bit more detail.

1. **Observe**: Identify the event, for instance, by collecting data of the market, competition, or customer behavior. That data has a time stamp, which means that the data reflects the situation as it is. Therefore, it's necessary to capture this data, at a high frequency in a continuous mode.

2. **Orient**: The event is place in context. Under what circumstances does the event occur? This will help in reaching a conscious decision – the business reflects on the event and the circumstances that have been observed and considers what is the best decision given the circumstances.

3. **Decide**: All potential outcomes are considered based on observations and the context that was studied during the orientation.

4. **Act**: The decision is executed, immediately followed by observing the outcomes.

All of this only works if there's appetite for change and willingness to adopt changes. That's culture. Culture is defined by people. The first task ahead is to identify the promoters, the sponsors, the laggards, and the blockers.

- Promoters

- Sponsors

- Laggards

- Blockers

Management of change often fails because of lack of communication and lack of commitment. Without transparent communication and the organization's commitment, change will never be adopted. Adoption is linked directly to culture and the appetite for change. That requires sponsorship and such can only be defined through a stakeholder map using the identification of the promoters, sponsors, laggards, and blockers. Next to this stakeholder map, we need strong leadership. Strong leadership starts with a shared vision. That vision must be meaningful, inspiring, and felt to be achievable. The organization must "feel" that the vision is real, compelling, and leading to a better future of the company and its customers. The shared vision is a necessity for alignment of all activities in an enterprise.

P. Senge writes in his book *The Fifth Discipline*: "In a corporation, a shared vision changes people's relationship with the company. It is no longer 'their company'; it becomes 'our company'. A shared vision is the first step in allowing people who mistrusted each other to begin to work together. It creates a common identity."

The vision is the navigating compass of the enterprise. It entails the enterprise's mission, carried by shared values. The strategy is the method to achieve the ambition that is set in the vision. Leaders are responsible for the clear communication of the vision, mission, and ambition, but more important, they should put trust in the organization to take ownership of the changes that will lead to the success that is envisioned. Only when vision, mission, and ambition are clear and shared, the organization will adopt and adapt to the changes. This is a process too. There's no way to turn around a complete enterprise just in one go. The adoption process starts with the coalition of the willing, the front-runners who support and share the vision and the business strategy. These are the promotors (actively promoting the change) and the sponsors (supporting the change). The promotors and the sponsors have a major task in empowering the teams to take ownership of the changes and to contribute to the success.

An agile organization is an organization where people in teams are empowered, enabling them to do what needs to be done, by allowing teams to decide for themselves based on their knowledge and skills The usage of this knowledge and skills must be stimulated to unleash the necessary creativity that we need in an innovative enterprise. One of the major tasks of the enterprise architect is to remove constraints, things that keep people from being or becoming creative. Any obstacle will stop the innovation and the flow of new ideas, but not having trust in the capabilities of teams will definitely kill the creative process and eventually put the enterprise out of business.

Note   Next to my full-time job as a principal consultant at Fujitsu and author – this is already 120% of my time – I also run a small consultancy firm under the name of Doppler Consultancy. The "O" in the name is presented as a cycle with three other Os representing observe, orientate, and operate, referring to OODA as well. The business as usual (keeping the lights on) is captured in operate, while observe and orientate focus on the continuous change of the future business. This cycle captures the principle of change management.

The enterprise architect plays a crucial role in this leadership. The enterprise architect is the bridge between the culture that focuses on keeping the lights on and a business that understands that needs to find a new light. That new light might be the North Star.

Putting It All Together in the Architectural Vision

A modern EA for digital transformation has to address the following topics. You will recognize all the attributes from the past chapters and sections.

Ambition, Vision, and Goals

Enterprises who have an EA are already quite mature. They have at least documented the origins of the enterprise and how the organization works together in creating products and services. When done right, the EA reflects the mission of the enterprise and enables achieving business goals in a structured approach that is implemented on all layers of the organization.

Now this enterprise is starting the digital transformation. That comes with a different ambition: to become a digital savvy enterprise that can quickly respond to changing customer needs, adopting new business models such as subscription-based and "anything as a service." Once more, you can't simply turn that huge ship around in one go, it must be done step by step, continuously learning from feedback. Maturity models can help with setting the ambition and defining the roadmap with the appropriate steps. The ambition is achieving maturity in digital.

Figure 4-4 represents the ambition of the digital enterprise. It's a more detailed view of the diagram that was presented in Chapter 3 showing the different tiers. It also shows how DevOps and agile fit in the mature enterprise architecture.

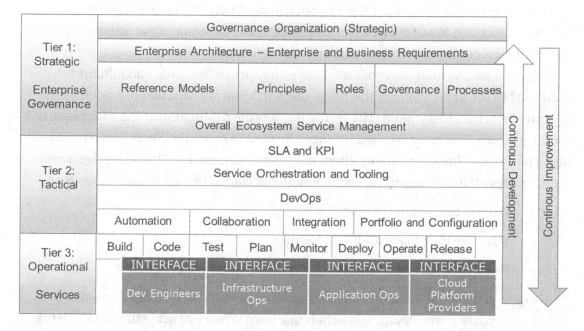

Figure 4-4. *A representation of an enterprise demarcation model*

The ambition is set on the highest tier: this is where new business models are set out as strategy for the entire enterprise. To support new business models, we can use reference models that are translated into principles: the guardrails of how the business is operated. Be aware that these must be business principles. Fundamental business principles are, for instance, knowing your industry and the competitors within that industry or delivering a high-quality product. But as important are these principles:

- Understand the financing structure.

- Understand the operational processes.

- Set the customer as priority.

These principles will evolve over time as the business grows – or matures.

The tactical tier is the layer where the business is translated into required services to fulfill the business. Since the enterprise will be part of a supply chain and with that of an ecosystem, it will need to find ways to do business with other entities. These ways are defined in agreements and contracts.

The operational tier is where we find Dev(Sec)Ops: it's where the execution of the plans, fulfilling the ambition, really takes shape. This means that everything in the strategic and tactical level must be actionable. That's where most EAs go off the rails: try to give a team the EA and ask them to build accordingly. Nothing will come out of it. Refer to the section about the DevSecOps principles to understand the activities in this layer and their connection to the tactic and strategic layer.

How can we use maturity models to guide enterprises in setting and fulfilling ambition? In the first chapter of this book, the North Star was discussed: a point where the enterprise puts its focus on. The North Star sets the destination of the enterprise, but not the journey. The latter is called strategy: the road to reach the North Star. That North Star is part of the ambition. Clarity about the ambition is crucial. The enterprise architect plays an important role in getting and defining that clarity, by asking these questions:

- What is the long-term vision?

- What are the objectives for midterm?

- How will it serve the customers?

Despite quite some literature, long term is not ten years. In the digital era, this is three to five years at maximum. Midterm is one year. When you get your teams to work agile in sprints of two to three weeks, there will be a dramatic disconnect if the enterprise sets long-term ambitions that spread over more than five years. The ambition will not be executable, or better said, actionable.

This also means that a transformation has to be set over a period that is actionable in short and mid-terms. The issue with most transformations is that they take way too much time. People "forget" what the ambition was and objectives get blurry. Maturity models can help in defining the transformation roadmap.

The Capability Maturity Model (CMM) is probably best known, describing where an organization stands in terms of software development. The principles that are used in CMM are commonly practiced in other models too, as you will learn later on in this section. The basic model is shown in Figure 4-5.

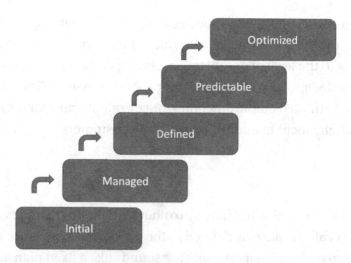

Figure 4-5. *Capability Maturity Model*

The basic level is initial that indicates that processes are not defined and tasks are mostly done ad hoc. The initial level is highly reactive. Organizations respond to events but have no insights of upcoming events or have processes that describe how to deal with those future events. As you have seen throughout this book, digital savvy companies must be on top of the game: they must know what their customers are after and be able to respond to changing market conditions fast. The business architecture must facilitate that. There must be processes that define how the enterprise captures the market demands and return that feedback to development of products and services.

The next level, managed, will not be sufficient too. Projects in managed are quite well defined, but the organization as a whole is still very reactive. Projects are managed, but not consistently throughout the company. Every project is on itself. There's not a one way of working that defines how projects are run in a consistent manner. Processes that are proactive and implemented through the entire enterprise and even applicable for ecosystems where enterprises are part of, are part of the defined level in the maturity model.

Levels 4 and 5 must be the ambition of every company, but they are hard to reach. At these levels outcomes of processes can and are quantitatively measured and even optimized, meaning that the enterprise can focus on improvement of the processes.

"Enterprise architecture (EA) practitioners are often frustrated by the gap between their experience and existing frameworks and, as a corollary, by the uncertain benefits, substantial overheads, and steep learning curves of a principled approach to EA." The quote is coming the Caminao blog (refer to `https://caminao.blog/knowledgeable-organizations/the-pagoda-playbook/`) where the "Pagoda Playbook" is presented as a toolkit for enterprise architects to start dealing with the maturity challenges of enterprises. Using the layered model of a Pagoda, it helps architects to iterate enterprise assets and projects to the level of optimization, aiming to leverage organizations from ad hoc and noncontrolled processes to repeatable processes. With defined and measurable processes in place with predictable outcomes, organizations can start automating these processes and shift the focus to adding value to their customers.

Strategy

Strategy is derived from ambition. There's no other way. Strategy defines the route to the North Star. Typically, strategy is defined as the actions the enterprise must take to achieve its ambition and realize its vision. That sounds like a fixed plan and usually that plan is set out over the course of multiple years. Enterprises still need to have that long-term vision to guide directions, but modern enterprises will be faced with the challenge that a strategy must be adapted all the times, since market conditions and customer behavior change all the times. The strategy itself must be agile and adaptive, ready for iterations of that strategy because there will be unpredicted events. There will be disruption. Enterprises must be prepared for that.

Once more, strategy is derived from ambition. That must be business ambition. Digital shift in itself is not a strategy, nor "cloud first" or equivalent statements. Digital shift and cloud are tools, ways to lead the enterprise to fulfill the business ambition. The ambition can be to become a leader in a specific industry in a certain area. In the strategy, the enterprise defines how it will achieve that ambition, for instance, by focusing completely on that specific industry and nothing else. Part of the strategy might be digitalization of product lines. Digitalization is not a goal on itself, but a way to reach the business goals.

This also means that the transformation and the change are not triggered by digitalization, but by business demands. That implies that the impact of transformation goes beyond digitalization: it transforms the business, with aid of digitalization.

Culture

We talked about the middle mud: the layer with managers who are responsible for operations. Operations must be stable. Change is a threat to stability. When operations are impacted by implemented changes, the operations layer typically gets to fix it. Isn't that what DevOps is supposed to be solving? Yes, it does. The truth however is that most enterprises only practice DevOps in Name Only (DINO). All too often there's still some form of a handover from developers to operators. Or worse, security is not involved in the DevOps teams.

Famous and likely very recognizable example, the company works in agile/SCRUM teams, in sprints of two to three weeks, using DevOps principles. Developers have worked on new features and now planning for release. Everything is tested following the promotion path: development, test, staging, and next release to production. For the final release some firewall settings must be altered to allow the new feature to function. The request is dropped to security – that takes one to two weeks to assess the request and decide to approve or deny. The first question that will come back to the team is probably: why do you need these ports to be opened or settings to be changed?

This is culture. Nothing else. It comes from fixed ideas in enterprises: "This is how we've done things for years." And it's coming from a hierarchical way of managing: "There's only one person responsible and that's the person who has the final say." Both do not work in agile organizations. Changing the culture starts with adopting collaboration as the working model. This model is characterized by working together in consensus. These teams have the "change spirit."

Enterprises do not succeed just by collaboration. Collaboration is not the only driver to adopting change. Competence has to be included: the enterprise that is willing to win, to beat the competition. Only companies that feel that competitors will be overhauling them will be "forced" to change. Lastly, cultivation is crucial in growing maturity in culture. Organizations that understand that they grow as their people grow. In these organizations, change is an "automatic" process. Growth comes automatically with adopting changes.

How can culture be included in architecture? That's a question that is very hard to answer. According to Edgar Schein (https://sites.psu.edu/global/2020/04/07/managing-organizational-change-lewin-schein/), change of culture is either caused by a severe crisis – think of major business disruption – or through evolution. The latter can be managed through three stages: unfreeze, change, and refreeze. The model, developed by Kurt Lewin, is shown in Figure 4-6.

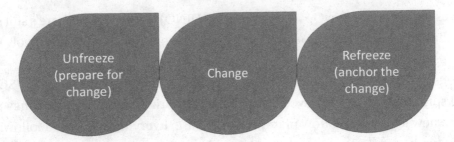

Figure 4-6. *Stages of change by Kurt Lewin*

Lewin uses the principle of "leveraging the power of small" in the first, unfreeze stage, starting with a group that feels the urgent need for change. It recognizes the fact that a lot of people in the organization are not willing to change, unless it's absolutely transparent how the change will also benefit them. The workforce needs to be motivated to accept the change. That's where the enterprise architect plays a significant role: in making the changes acceptable through easy-to-adopt processes and – there it finally is – easy-to-use technology. This includes digital inclusion, more specific digital literacy, and digital well-being: making people feel comfortable.

That's in essence where every transformation is about: adopting change and making people feel comfortable with it. An enterprise who can achieve that is growing in maturity. Maturity goes hand in hand with adoption.

Transformation Approach (CMO to FMO)

Any transformation approach that starts with implementing new technology will fail. There has to be a sense of urgency and a willingness to change. Only then, the impact of transformation will be adopted. But, only when the rationales for the transformation, objectives, and strategy are very clearly communicated to all stakeholders. An adoption roadmap is a good tool to guide this process.

First question to be answered is, does the organization want to adopt the change? Yes, of course. Or was that too easy? Remember what we said about a culture in an organization. Not everyone is probably willing to adopt changes. The adoption process will either start bottom-up or top-down. Top-down usually means that an organization is forced to adopt, which is hardly ever a success. In bottom-up there will likely be a group of workers that initiate the change and starts the adoption process, showing that a change is improving the business.

The whole process starts with knowing where the company is today, the current mode of operation (CMO). Together with all stakeholders, the desired state is defined: the future mode. This will reveal where change is needed and what the transformation should be focusing on. One more time, don't focus on systems. Focus on the organization and moreover the adaptivity of the organization. An adaptive organization matches its products and services continuously to the market demands and, by doing that, optimizes the usage of resources. The challenge is that an adaptive enterprise is constantly changing and that requires agility and flexibility. They can shift business priorities quickly and adjust operations along with it. So, that's our north star: the adaptive enterprise.

We can identify four main stages in the transformation plan.

- **Discovery**: In this stage we're creating an inventory of every single asset that an enterprise has. This also includes the organization itself – what are the business lines, units, who are the stakeholders, and what resources does the organization have. Architects can use reference models to streamline the discovery results, creating comprehensible reference maps of the business model, business functionality, capabilities, applications, and lastly the technological platforms.

- **Assessment**: In this stage the results of the discovery phase are reviewed. What is crucial in this stage is to assess the business criticality. Are processes, resources, applications, and so forth required to operate the business and deliver the products that customers have a demand for? This exercise will eventually lead to the target architecture, the future mode. Since our north star is the adaptive organization, architects must challenge the need for every asset. The risk of tied-up capital, obsolete resources, and overhead processes are significant and will definitely slow down the transformation and blur the north star.

- **Planning**: We have an inventory of our CMO. Our ambition and goals are set out in the North Star. Now, it's time to plan all activities that lead toward that north star. With this the maturity model can be a great help since it guides in setting the priorities. We can't stress it enough: from an EA perspective, the priority is not in implementing new technology.

- **Execution**: This is the stage where activities are deployed. It's important that during execution activities are measured and validated against the ambition and the derived goals. Any activity that turns out not to add value to the realization of ambition and goals should be eliminated.

Figure 4-7 shows the high-level stages of the transformation approach.

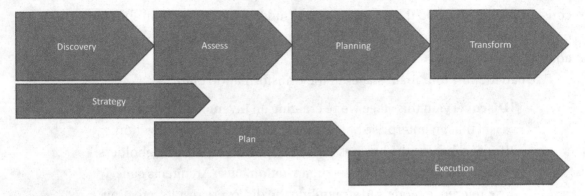

***Figure 4-7.** High-level stages of transformation*

In summary, the transformation approach must contain the following:

- **Ambition, vision, goals**: The "what"

- **Strategy**: The "how"

- **Plan**: An overview of the teams and the projects

- **Planning**: A realistic, achievable timeline

Under "ambition," we noticed that maturity models can help in transformation. Let's take a specific model to work with: Acatech. Acatech defines four areas of transformation. The model is designed for Industry 4.0, but you will surely recognize all the principles.

- Resources

  - Digital capability

  - Structural communication

- Information systems
  - Information processing
  - Integration
- Organizational structures
  - Organic internal organization
  - Dynamic cooperation in the network
- Culture
  - Willingness to change
  - Social collaboration

Based on the current capabilities of these areas, organizations can plan their development path of processes and organizational structure to increase the maturity. The index itself has six stages of all maturities combined:

1. **Computerization**: This includes the use of information technology to run processes in a company. This is the digital capability of the enterprise.

2. **Connectivity**: This is connectivity between resources. How do they work together?

3. **Visibility**: Resources have to be able to see what is happening in real time.

4. **Transparency**: Resources must understand why it is happening. There must be common understanding of events and why events occur.

5. **Predictability**: Resources must know what will happen so they can prepare for change in forecasting. This is key in the adoption process.

6. **Adaptability**: Resources must be enabled to adapt to the change and take decisions to execute the change.

This is a maturity model; hence, the adaptive organization is the highest level of maturity that an enterprise can reach. To reach that level, all other levels must be fulfilled: from collaboration to a common understanding of events and being able to forecast events that eventually lead to fast adaptation and adoption of change.

Resources

In architecture, we usually refer to "things" if we talk about resources. In cloud, resources are anything that is required to run a service: servers, databases, load balancers, routers, and storage appliances. But the most important resource of the enterprise are people. Digital transformation is about human transformation: we concluded that already in one of the previous sections. Unfortunately, enterprise architects easily tend to forget about their most critical "asset" – the people working in and for the enterprise.

We discussed the organization itself: unbundling and rebundling in small teams – micro-enterprises – that are close to the customer. It's making the organization agile. Agile organizations have to be open and transparent. People in the organization will be faced with changes, and this will impact their way of working in the enterprise. To some this will be an opportunity, but to others this will be a threat. In *Unlocking Agility*, Jorgen Hesselberg quotes Dean Leffingwell, author of *Scaled Agile Framework (SAFe)*: "If nobody wants to quit when you're going through a significant transformation, you're clearly not doing it right!"

There will be people struggling with change. This requires coaching, helping these people in understanding the change and the need for the transformation. The challenge is that agile organizations require people with agile mindsets. Hesselberg refers to this as the growth mindset. Organizations must be ready and willing to operate in a VUCA world (volatility, uncertainty, complexity, ambiguity) and so do people who work in these organizations. This requires people that always want to learn and, by doing so, grow. Hence, the growth mindset.

How does an enterprise architect incorporate this in an architecture? By creating an architecture that allows people to grow. This is the architecture that allows for iteration, to try things and learn from it, an architecture that allows for adaptation. And of course, it's a cultural thing. Enterprises will need to adopt an open, transparent, learning culture that is diverse so that new ideas can freely float, leading to innovations and beating the disruption.

Technology with Intrinsic Security and Cost Awareness

Finally, we're getting to technology. It's the last domain the enterprise architect should be concerned about. In practice, a lot of enterprise architects are acting more as solution architects, meaning that their daytime job mainly consists of finding (technical) solutions to problems of an enterprise. That's why most enterprises get the implementation of technology wrong.

What happens in most cases? It starts with the technology, service, a specific tool, or piece of software that is purchased and is considered to be a must for people to improve the outcome of their work. And, enterprise architects are also due to this. What should enterprise architects do?

First of all, assess if the technology change is really needed. Does it improve productivity and outcomes for the enterprise? Then ask what impact the implementation will have, taken into account the capabilities of the enterprise and the skills of the workforce. Have prerequisites been met to implement the new technology and is proper support arranged for?

But the most important thing in implementing new technology: it should fix a problem. This can be any problem. It might be nonfunctioning applications that are hindering people from doing their job, but also the enterprise that isn't able to sell its products. These are the cases where enterprise architects must find solutions. Technology can be a great help. The EA must be the guide in searching for solutions, coaching teams to find these solutions and make sure that all prerequisites are met in implementing these. That's driving innovation.

Guiding teams in finding solutions to problems also means that you have to train teams in thinking security and making them aware of costs. In simple words, teams must know that every decision that they make comes with a consequence. That certainly counts for introducing new technology. New software and tools must be assessed against the security policies of the enterprise. Next, does it comply with budgeting rules? Does the new technology add value to the enterprise? If so, there's likely a proper business case, but in all cases the return on investment must be within the financial boundaries of the enterprise. Business agility doesn't equal unlimited credits – not in security, not in costs.

We can wrap it all up in a model that will set the contours of the modern EA, guiding the digital transformation. The model is shown in Figure 4-8.

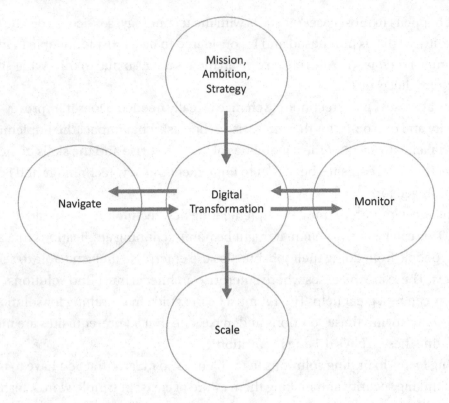

Figure 4-8. *Model for digital transformation*

The model is characterized by four stages:

- Strategy
- Navigate
- Monitor
- Scale

These four stages contain

- Ambition set in the North Star
- Strategic change management
- Navigate in a resilient, stable, but adaptive environments using DevSecOps

- Culture with collaborating and continuously learning teams (growth mindset)

- Monitor: customer feedback (Voice of the Customer)

In the next section we will learn how to translate this into actionable patterns.

Modern Architecture Patterns

In the previous chapter we drew a plan to create an architecture vision. This vision includes every aspect of the enterprise: the ambition of the enterprise, the organization, the required resources, and finally the technology. From the ambition and the vision, the enterprise architect now faces the next challenge: creating the comprehensive architecture patterns. Why does he or she needs to do that? The ambition and the vision must be actionable, executable. Teams must be able to work on their respective tasks and these tasks are derived from patterns. Also remember the OODA principles that we discussed: the enterprise will be working iterative and conditions might change along the way, requiring a recalibration – even of the ambition if necessary.

In defining patterns, we can use reference models. You will notice that these follow the principles of TOGAF: business, data, applications, and technology:

- **Business models**: Business models provide quick insight into the essence of an organization. It's particularly suitable for facilitating discussions about the strategic position of the organization, and as such, it's the starting point for the architecture of an organization and the core activities of the enterprise. These must be worked out in more detail into business functions that are necessary to enable these core activities. The model contains the following:

  - **Core competencies**: What are we good at?

  - **Strategic partners**: How do we need to be good in our core competences?

  - **Cost model**: What does it cost to be good at it?

  - **Customer segments**: For who do we need to be good at it?

  - **Value propositions**: The proof that we're good.

- **Information model (data)**: This model is used to show where data is and who the owner is of that data. Next, we can use this model to show how data can be used in systems, determining what relevant data is and how it can be transferred and applied in a secure way.

- **Business processes**: This includes all activities necessary to achieve a certain result, including activities that are part of the support or business operations. In addition, operational management is also part of the business processes, so that the execution of the activities is coordinated. Business processes can be executed in response to a specific event that occurs (event-driven) or executed at set times.

- **Application functions**: This model describes what application supports what business process. There must be a one-to-one mapping of application functions to business processes. An application function that is not linked to a business process has no use and is obsolete. Obviously, business processes must be linked one-to-one with the core competencies of the enterprise. Processes that are not linked are considered to be overhead and will only generate costs without a clearly defined outcome to the performance of the enterprise – or adding value to the customers.

- **Application artifacts**: This is the connection with the technology layer of the architecture. In application artifacts all components of the applications are listed. The most complete and rigid form of it is the SBOM: the software bill of material. The SBOM lists all components used to build a specific piece of software, including versions and patch levels. Remember that security is intrinsic: SBOM is mainly used to capture possible vulnerabilities in software and software supply chains.

- **Application platforms**: This is the technology layer and describes where applications are hosted and operated. These can be public cloud platforms such as Azure and AWS, or on-premises datacenters. The model describes all components that are used to build the platform: servers, databases, storage, network, and security perimeter equipment such as firewalls.

These reference models will help the enterprise architect to define the value streams in the enterprise. If there's one lesson you will get out of this book, let it be this one: stop thinking in architecture layers. Start thinking in value streams. Yes, an architecture requires structure and that's what layers will provide, but it won't help in defining the value for customers. The problem with customers is that they are humans. The problem with humans is that their behavior constantly changes. That is hardly ever reflected in EA.

Value streams focus on outcome: a desired state. Desired by who? By the customer, but also by any stakeholder in the enterprise ecosystem. The desired outcome is translated into a value proposition. The proposition is delivered through the enterprise capabilities. The capabilities are defined by the enterprise artifacts: planning, resources, systems, and people. The stakeholder sets the delivery of a value proposition in motion by a request. Next, the resources to deliver that proposition must be assigned to that request. This sequence sets the patterns for modern architecture.

So, what do we need to fulfill the value streams? The Business Architecture Metamodel of the Business Architecture Guild (refer to www. businessarchitectureguild.org/) provides practical answers:

1. **Capabilities**: These are the business functionalities, what the enterprise does. Important to remember is that a capability has an outcome.

2. **Information**: The data that the business needs to fulfill the functionalities, the data that is needed to build the value proposition.

3. **Planning the organization**: We need an organization that really brings producers and consumers together in optimized collaboration. This organization is cross-functional, cross-border, and functions in ecosystems. Refer to the previous chapter where we discussed the concept of micro-enterprises.

4. **Stakeholder mapping**: All stakeholders must actively be involved in defining strategy, tactics, development, and operations. All activities are key in delivering the value proposition.

5. **Strategy**: The strategy is declarative in terms of objectives and goals that all stakeholders must comply with. It sets the course of the enterprise, but also allows navigation when circumstances change. The OODA loop will help in navigating.

We haven't answered one question yet: how do we create patterns? By starting with the broadest scope (ambition) and then narrow it down to the level of the teams and the tools they can use to build the value propositions. Value streams will help the architect to narrow the scope down to the level of principles and practices.

Figure 4-9 shows the principle of building patterns.

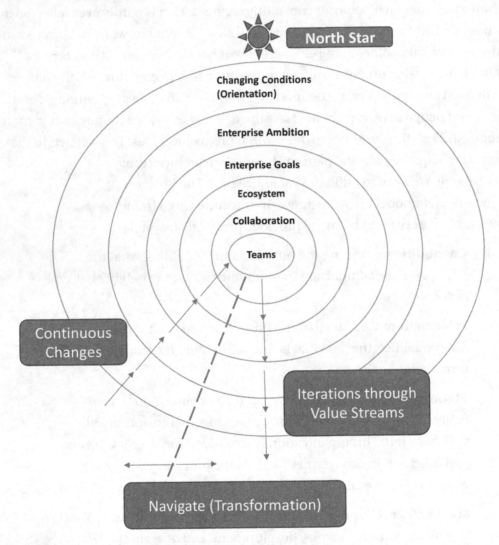

Figure 4-9. *Model for building enterprise patterns*

A pattern is a method to describe a solution to a problem. To build a solution, the architect uses building blocks. The pattern will tell the architect how to use the building block to create the solution that provides an answer to the problem. Since it is a pattern, this solution is repeatable.

So, the first thing the architect "needs" is a problem: what are we trying to solve? However, every problem has a context. The context is the precondition under which the problem exists and to what the pattern offers a solution for. The challenge in our modern, VUCA world is that these conditions continuously change and thus teams are continuously iterating the solutions.

According to TOGAF, a pattern "expresses a fundamental structural organization or schema for software systems. It provides a set of predefined subsystems, specifies their responsibilities, and includes rules and guidelines for organizing the relationships between them." But this doesn't cover our modern architecture patterns: we need to include the continuity of the changing conditions that impact solutions and thus our patterns. We need a continuous orientation. By observing these changes, teams must navigate through iterations, yet keep the focus on the enterprise ambition. In terms of value streams, teams must continuously be challenged to maximize the value.

The value chain is a good tool to help teams in creating, sustaining, and maximizing value. The value chain represents the business processes to create value for customers. The value chain as defined by Michael Porter contains five pillars:

- Inbound logistics

- Operations

- Outbound logistics

- Marketing and sales

- Services

Basically, it tells how customers know of products (solutions) and how these products are sold and delivered to customers.

The value stream represents the steps the business must take to provide a solution to the customer. It provides answer to the questions:

- For who is this solution?

- What is the solution?

- How is the solution delivered to customers?

- What does the customer gain from the solution?

- Why is the solution better than other solutions, given performance indicators?

- Does the solution add to the business strategy, given budgets and costs?

In defining actionable steps in the value stream, the architect must narrow the scope down from the observations of the customer needs, map these to the enterprise ambitions and goals, and next define tasks that teams need to perform to contribute to the solution.

In summary, the architect constantly works with these four questions:

- What is the purpose of the business (why are we doing business)?

- How do we do business?

- For who are we doing business?

- With who are we doing business?

This will drive the navigation and the transformation.

In continuous architecture the answers are validated against the quality attributes. Are we delivering solutions that add value to the customer? Is the solution cost-effective? Secure? Does it perform well? Is it robust and reliable? Is it easy to use? Is it easy to manage and operate? Is it configurable? And, most important, is it scalable?

Every single architecture must address these questions. Again and again, with every single change to the solution because of changed conditions. Observe and orientate: Are we still on track to our North Star? Keeping on track also means avoiding antipatterns, to be discussed in the next section.

Avoiding Antipatterns in Enterprise Architecture

The biggest antipattern is the EA itself. The big overarching architecture spanning the entire business, portfolio, and organization. Antipatterns are events that will lead to new inhibitions and therefore must be avoided.

- Starting without a core mission

- Doing EA from the architecture ivory tower (not transparent)

- Keeping silos alive

- Embracing the middle mud

- Assuming it already has been done

- Assuming the new product/feature already exists (killing innovation)

- Assuming scalability

Continuous architecture mentions a few more typical enterprise antipatterns. First, the definition of an antipattern is a standard, default approach to issues resulting in undesired outcomes. Hence, the default decision is probably the biggest antipattern: "we've always done it this way." This is devastating to the innovative drive of any company and its people. Decisions always must be challenged: Are there better ways to deal with an issue? This doesn't mean that an enterprise shouldn't have standardized processes. Without standardization automation is not possible. But let's turn this around: everything standard should be automated. Innovation and agility require creativity. Creativity needs options. The default decision will always lead to the path of least friction and typically this will lead to status quo and technical debt.

The enterprise architect, again, has a big task in avoiding these antipatterns. Since they're involved in the ambition, mission, and strategy of the enterprise, they must assemble stakeholders and challenge them. A way to do this is by working through storyboards. How do stakeholders envision the journey toward the North Star, the goals, and the overall ambition?

Key is communication about the processing of this input: the enterprise architect has to communicate with all stakeholders, being absolute transparent in the status of the architecture. He might need different channels for this, but an example of collecting input and reporting on the architectural status is the way the Dutch enterprise architecture for higher education is presented (HORA: `https://hora.surf.nl/index.php/Hoofdpagina`): a comprehensive portal and a wiki page that guides stakeholders through all architectural artifacts, given a specific stakeholder view (business functionality, applications, technology). Figure 4-10 shows a screenshot of the landing page.

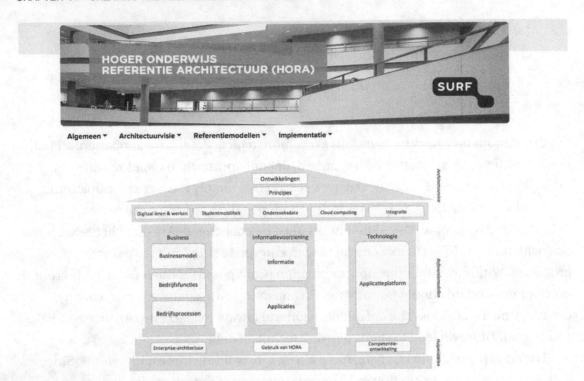

Figure 4-10. *Example of a wiki page for enterprise architecture*

Here the architecture is presented as a house. The three pillars standing on the architecture foundation represent the business, data, and technology. The roof contains development and principles, providing the guardrails for digital, cloud, data, and integration.

We've worked out how we can create an architecture that allows for agility. The biggest challenge is yet to come and it's where most companies fail: scaling. This is the central topic of the next chapter.

Summary

The modern enterprise architecture is an architecture that allows for business agility. Businesses must be enabled to respond fast to changing demands. We need a floating architecture that allows the enterprise to navigate toward its ambition: it needs to change course quickly, if necessary, but still head for the final destination, the North Star.

In this chapter we looked at various methods and tools to create that architecture. The continuous architecture framework is a good start, but we also discussed agile methods such as DevSecOps. The risk we face as architects is that we start focusing on technology, where in digital transformation the real challenge lies in transforming the mindset. Organizations and people working for those organization must have the growth mindset. Creating that mindset and transforming the culture is part of architecture too. But the most important question that we must answer in creating architecture is, what does it do for our business, for our customers? We've looked at all the artifacts, capabilities, and skills that are required to build that architecture.

Once we have the architecture, we must be able to scale it. It's the central topic for the next chapter.

CHAPTER 5

Scaling the Business with Enterprise Architecture

This chapter is about scaling. We will look at reasons why enterprises must be ready to scale, both up and down. The key is in the hands of the customer: the enterprise that is able to forecast the demands of the customer will be able to forecast its business and make sure that capacity and capabilities are utilized in an optimized manner. Making optimal use of capacity and capabilities is the essence of business scaling.

Why Businesses Must Be Scalable

We all know the stories. Amazon starting in a garage. The start of Apple with the Apple I, invented by Steve Wozniak and Steve Jobs. Even the biggest enterprises once started small. The art is to scale the business once you have a product, or a service established. The success of enterprises lies in scaling.

But what is scaling? The risk is that a business thinks too easily about scaling. It's not as simple as multiplying the product or the service. A business must think about the supply chain, the required resources and capacity of operations, distribution channels, and the associated costs. Scaling comes at a cost. Scaling the business is about growth and expansion, but a company will only grow if it has mastered the art of scaling. Scaling might even include investments, so that the enterprise is ready to scale when the market demands for it. It often means that the enterprise already has to invest in the capacity. The problem there is that the capacity might be underutilized for a while. That's where most of the costs are generated: from idle capacity. It must be considered in terms of the business case. The overall business model must be able to adapt to changes and scale along with these changes.

© Jeroen Mulder 2023
J. Mulder, *Modern Enterprise Architecture*, https://doi.org/10.1007/978-1-4842-9066-8_5

We must clarify one important aspect in debating scalability. It includes growth and expansion by scaling up or scaling out. Simple explanation: Scaling up is expanding the resource, scaling out is adding more units of the resource. For example, if we scale up a server, we increase the processing power and memory in that server so that one server can handle more load. With scale out, we add more servers, spreading the load over multiple servers. The same principle can be applied to other resources, yes – even people. Simple example: asking a team member to work more hours (scale up) or adding more people to the team (scale out). Having said that, please do keep seeing team members as people and not as resources.

But there's an opposite possibility as well: scaling down. The enterprise needs to be ready to scale down when markets drop. Then it must be absolutely clear what the impact is. No business wants to get in the situation where it has to lay off personnel or rapidly depreciate resources. It must be prepared for various scenarios. That's scalability.

Every enterprise will have a baseline to run its operations. That might be a minimal number of machines or staff to run the business and still make some profit. From that baseline, we can apply scenarios to define the required level of scaling. The technique to do this is called scenario planning and – you've guessed it – the enterprise architect has an important role in this.

Every organization is confronted with different events on a daily basis. Some of these events are predictable, others are not. Remember that in the previous chapter we talked about the OODA loop: observe, orient, decide, and act. OODA allows organizations to continuously calibrate the direction of the enterprise. Have circumstances changed, forcing the enterprise to change its course? OODA should be part of the scenario planning: enterprises can and must plan for various scenarios, but at the same time be agile in adapting the course and switch scenarios. However, some events can cause a drastic turn in business in both the short and long term. That is why it is necessary for organizations to be prepared for future events. This preparation drives the scale – and the required effort of scaling – of the enterprise and its operations.

With scenario planning, organizations are able to develop their strategies, products, and services and possibly adapt them to an ever-changing world: the VUCA world, that is. The world is volatile, uncertain, complex, and ambiguous. VUCA makes it even harder to set course and to stay on course. We already drew the conclusion that a floating architecture must enable the enterprise to navigate in changing courses. Scenarios allow an organization to make better choices in the event of problems or changes. In this way, an organization knows what to take into account and which decisions will ultimately work out the best.

What causes the events, forcing the enterprise to change? Typically, we talk about DESTEP: Demographics, Economics, Social affairs, Technology, Ecology, and Politics. Indeed, most of these are coming from the outside in. Causes are external but do heavily influence the business and the enterprise itself. They might and probably will force the enterprise to change strategy, ambitions, goals, and the direction.

An example will help in understanding this. At time of writing, many industries in Western Europe face the issue of lack of resources. Resources can be materials – think of chips – but also personnel. Let's take the shortfall of chips: What was the cause of this shortfall? Demand for chips was still high, but the delivery of chips became a massive problem for many industries, for instance, car manufacturing. Zero COVID policies in China resulting in lengthy lockdowns of important technology hubs in China were one of the causes. Worldwide distribution of chips halted. On top of that came the war in Ukraine, resulting in economical very uncertain times. Due to shortfall of chips, car manufacturing was heavily disrupted with enormous delays in the delivery of new cars. The urgency for changing course hardly ever comes from internal issues in enterprises. In almost every case, the events are coming from the outside: external issues that hit the company.

Working with Scenario Planning

Scenario planning allows organizations to think about how they can still be successful in different scenarios. Scenario planning forces organizations to think about the future in an effective and structured way – structured, since enterprises must follow a number of steps in planning.

1. Find the most important reason for uncertainty.

2. Identify the business factors that could be affected by the uncertainty.

3. Identify the most critical reasons for uncertainty and the affected business factors.

4. Narrow scenario planning to these critical factors.

5. Detail the scenarios to full extent.

It's impossible to cater for every event that will happen in the future, but it is possible to think of events that are likely to happen and will affect the business. These events can be good or bad, but in all cases the business must be able to adapt to the effects of these events. Outcomes of scenario planning could be questions such as identifying the market to hire staff – or in case of "bad events" prepare for cutting costs. In the scenario planning, we need to think of the "how" can we cut costs by stopping contracts with external suppliers, by outtasking (indeed, in that case, we're initiating a contract with an external supplier), or worst case, by laying off staff? All of this has a scaling effect for the entire business: up or down.

There are a few things that we must understand before we start defining HOW to scale the business. For instance, scaling is not the same thing as growth. It's the reason why we underline the fact that scaling can be both up or down.

Scalability describes the capability of a business to breathe with the business. If sales go up, the enterprise needs to be able to spin up more production capacity and still perform well in terms of, for instance, financial results. But, the other way around is equally true. If sales go down, then the enterprise must be able to decrease production and still be able to perform, for instance, without losses.

So, scaling is mainly about two things, two parameters: capability and capacity. Both require a strategy, a plan, and planning. If in scenario 1, sales are boosting and the business is growing rapidly, does the enterprise have the capabilities and the capacity to cater for that expansion? And what are the mitigating plans if sales drop? (What are the reasons for that?) In either scenario, there will be customers that expect delivery. The good news is that as an outcome of digital transformation, technology has become available to enable scaling and still control costs in case of expansion or decrease.

But how do you determine the level of scaling? That's unfortunately not an exact science. It's first of all very much depending on the Voice of the Customer and "sensing" when the customer will be demanding new products, features of product, and services. Capturing that voice is crucial; we will learn why having marketing and sales is important in the process of scaling. The enterprise needs marketing and sales to capture that voice, to push for brand recognition, and to close new acquisitions. The next step is knowing if and when the enterprise is ready to scale; the first one is measuring if the organization is ready to adopt and handle the workloads.

Here's the big difference between growth and scaling. Growth is the business increasing sales and revenue. Scaling up is being able to adopt and handle growth. Scaling down is being able to handle decrease in revenue, but still maintaining a sound business. Knowing when and how to scale is therefore strongly depending on being able to predict the market.

- Is there demand for products and services that the enterprise has in its portfolio?

- Are these products and services continuously updated and upgraded, given the market trends?

- Is staff able to keep up, also in terms of knowledge and growing their skills to innovate products and services? In short, does the enterprise and all of its employees have a growth mindset?

- Does the enterprise have a growth mindset and is it willing to, as an example, hire staff with the right skills if the market demands so?

- Does the enterprise know what skills are required? Can you forecast the required capacity?

Then there's a difference between scaling up and out. If sales and revenue go up but the enterprise is able to cater for this without the requirement of extra capacity, then the enterprise is scaling out. If growth is forcing to add capacity, then we are scaling up. In the latter case, there will be investments involved to onboard that additional capacity. The enterprise needs to have finances in place to cater for that.

But be aware that if business is going down because of events (also remember our VUCA world and DESTEP principles), the enterprise must also be able to absorb these finances without the risk of creating issues in solvency, cash flow, and creditability. It must all be assessed in the scenarios.

Enabling Development Speed

There is a simple rule of thumb when it comes to developing speed. You need to focus and avoid distractions. In essence, there are two major tactics to increase the development speed and enable scaling:

1. Get rid of toil with lean operations. Toil is the expression that is used for something that takes a lot of laborious effort. We will get to Site Reliability Engineering (SRE) where toil is used to identify tedious tasks that can and must be automated.

2. Set clear goals for development.

The one doesn't go without the other. How do we achieve this?

1. **Define clear expectations**: It was discussed intensively in this book already, but enterprises must have a clear goal and strategy. This includes setting clear expectations to all stakeholders: when does the enterprise expect what? This must be clearly communicated to development teams, to start with. Timeframes must be realistic and achievable, but with room for overperformance. One goal is to have a minimum in toil: toil will put a heavy claim on resources. Enterprises who want to speed up delivery and be ready for scaling must first focus on lean operations. We will explore this further in this section.

2. **Expand the team in quality**: More doesn't necessarily mean better or faster. Improving development and innovation speed isn't a matter of getting more resources in but getting resources to work smarter and getting the right resources with the right skills and capabilities. This should be adaptable. There's no need for a modern enterprise to have every single skill and capability available within the enterprise itself: when specific skills or capabilities are required, enterprises can also get these from outside the enterprise. But, there must be arrangements within the ecosystem of the enterprise to realize this. It's the same principle as with supply chain management. The enterprise itself is the core with the critical resources to keep business going, the adaptivity in development and innovation is something that can be elevated in the ecosystem. Lastly, team members share responsibility but have to focus on their tasks.

3. **Become truly agile**: Focus on the outcome of a project. Release
   a minimum viable product (MVP) as soon as possible and start
   iterating and improving from there. Shape the team according
   to the iterations since every iteration will come with specific
   demands for skills, as demands for the end stage of the product
   will also alter per Voice of the Customer.

4. **Be firm and cut your backlog**: Reducing toil also means cutting
   down the backlog. How many tasks can a team really manage in
   one iteration? Everything that is not related to the product must be
   eliminated from the backlog. Leaving it there will be an invitation
   to start looking at these tasks. The problem is that backlogs get
   stuffed with tasks that are not time critical or even critical to the
   business. Always check and validate with the business goals and
   the strategy. If it's not contributing to achieving the goals and
   fulfilling the strategy, leading to added value to the enterprise, it
   shouldn't be on the backlog.

5. **Practice shift-left**: This is really a matter of trust, although
   shift-left is often referred to testing procedures: performing
   tests as early as possible in development projects. Shift-left also
   means shifting responsibility to the teams. Set the goals and
   expectations, define the product, and let the teams think of how
   they will manage. However, this implies that teams have KPIs,
   key performance indicators. KPIs should not be about number
   of hours or lines of code, but about accomplishing the tasks
   and delivering the product in time and according to customer
   demands. The most important KPI is the happy customer.

So, we need to get rid of toil and we need focus. One major mistake enterprises
make is focusing on the wrong goals. The goal should be business agility and innovation,
constantly capturing the Voice of the Customer. But a lot of enterprises focus on cost. We
can illustrate this with an example. Part of the digital transformation of the enterprise is
migrating to the cloud. The question is, why does the enterprise want to move workloads
to cloud? What is the rationale behind that? Going to the cloud is not a strategy, after all.
That's a statement. The strategy is the reason why development in cloud would benefit
the enterprise and moreover its customers.

"Let's go to 'the cloud' because it's cheaper." This is something we hear too often in many organizations. If money is your main motivation to migrate business functions to the cloud, then by all means don't do it. Innovation is a much better argument to do it.

Firstly, "the cloud" doesn't exist. Just like "the Internet" doesn't exist. What does exist are shared services, provided by third parties. Businesses purchase these services as platform as a service (PaaS) or software as a service (SaaS). The big advantage of PaaS, but especially SaaS, is that as a customer you don't really have to worry about the technical side of the service and delivery. The only thing that's important is whether the functionality meets the needs of your organization. The software and the underlying technical requirements are the responsibility of the service provider.

So why is this such a big advantage? Well, because it frees up manpower. Expensive and scarce manpower. By purchasing services subscription-based, an organization no longer has to maintain them itself. This creates space to do other things. Manpower – human resources – is the most important aspect in scaling.

Some companies believe that manpower that is "freed up" is no longer needed at all. The cloud, they argue, is therefore "cheaper." But that's a fallacy. Because by scaling down on human capital, companies also give up their power to innovation. It's quite simple: to innovate you need – good – people.

An interesting thought though is whether we still need operators. Sid Palas – who calls himself DevOps specialist, mind the extra "o" – sent out a remarkable tweet in July 2020 claiming that DevOps was dead. Developers don't want to be bothered with managing infrastructure, but companies still need to control that infrastructure. The answer to this problem: platform engineering. To put this very simple, design and build tools and workflows that enable self-service capabilities to build products, in most cases this would be software. Shift-left to the max: freeing up developers completely and release them from the burden operations.

It's not a bad idea at all. We live in exciting times, for any business. Customer demands are changing at a breakneck pace: it's what this whole book is about. It's up to any company to keep up, listen to this changing demand, and translate it to high-quality products and services. And still, that might not be enough. Many companies go the extra mile, by sensing what the customer demand is going to be and anticipating to that situation. If you do that, you are innovating. You need all the creativity that you can get in the company and have as little people stuck in ops as possible. Roles of developers and engineers will change dramatically, the topic of the final chapter of this book.

In fact, every company these days should be in a permanent "beta" state. By constantly challenging itself, do our products still meet our customers' expectations? What is it that our customer needs tomorrow? Are we still relevant tomorrow? Capturing of this "Voice of the Customer" is crucial to any company; we can't stress this enough.

This can even lead to products that the customer didn't even know it needed. For example, Apple has grown beyond all dreams by doing the above. They managed to create a demand with their iPods and iPhones. This is something very few companies have succeeded in.

The power to innovate requires brainpower. People. People who should not be dealing with the continuous maintenance of systems. That part should mainly be left to the systems themselves. This is the core idea of Site Reliability Engineering (SRE), a phenomenon introduced by Google. To be able to continuously innovate with new services, the company decided that it should automate standard processes as much and as far as possible.

If at Google a new service requires too much maintenance and therefore manpower, the service is referred back to the drawing board and the engineers get the assignment to further automate it. This is how you feed innovation: to free up time for innovation, you will have to remove all of the toil. Cloud technology offers plenty of possibilities to do this, if used properly.

As long as you keep thinking about these questions:

- Why am I migrating something to the cloud?

- How do I make the best use of cloud services? (*Spoiler: A lift and shift from servers to cloud is rarely a good solution.*)

- What will it ultimately yield?

- Does it produce room for innovation?

If we have done that and answered these questions, we are ready for the next step. We have implemented a platform that allows the business to scale, but that's not enough. We have only dealt with the technological side of scaling. The real challenge is yet to come, a challenge in which a lot of companies fail. It's the topic of the next section.

Why Scaling Fails and How to Solve It

The first part of the question is easy to answer. Scaling is depending on proper functioning of chains and a chain is as strong as its weakest link. We will explain using an example.

Something that has become quite popular over the past years are delivery services for groceries. One interesting concept is the service where the groceries are packed as ingredients for a specific meal. Subscribers receive a recipe and all the required ingredients to prepare the meal according to the recipe. For instance, the recipe is for making a pasta with tomato-based sauce. It includes minced meat, herbs, the pasta, and of course the tomatoes as the base for the sauce. These ingredients come from different suppliers. The meat is coming from a meat company (depending on delivery of animals by farmers) and the vegetables from selected greenhouses. All ingredients are delivered to a central warehouse where they get packaged per group of subscribers in a specific region. From the warehouse the packages are distributed to larger hubs and from there to the individual subscribers.

Now, what happens if only one link is broken in this chain? If the greenhouse fails to deliver tomatoes because of growing demand, the whole chain stops. It might be fixed by switching to another or an extra greenhouse (with the same quality of tomatoes), but there will be a delay. If it happens more than once, this will have an impact on the experience of the customer, resulting in negative reviews and with the ultimate result that business will go down.

Worse, the company is not able to get the packages distributed at all due to logistic issues. A distributing partner might not have enough personnel to deliver the packages to the customer. The company might be able to scale in terms of ingredients, but if the logistics fail, scaling will become problematic if not impossible.

Companies must think about the entire chain in terms of scaling, but too often a link is missed and scaling fails.

Failing scaling in supply chain is one reason but scaling also fails in terms of the organization itself, in human resources. We talked about it in the previous section. Does the organization have enough staff and, even more important, enough staff available with the right skills and capabilities? The first question an enterprise should ask itself is if it needs all the staff available within the enterprise. The answer is probably not. In the previous chapters, we discussed the model of micro-enterprises. If we unbundle and rebundle the organization in micro-enterprises who can use other micro-enterprises in the ecosystem, scaling becomes easier. But, the same principles as in supply chain management do apply.

Organizations must become adaptive. Based on the terms of delivery, it must identify what skills and capabilities are required to execute the delivery. Prerequisite to this is that the ecosystem has resources available.

With that, we might have a solution to fix the issue of failing organizational scalability.

This is a good point to have one more look at the concept of micro-enterprises. We've learned that scaling is not just about a technological platform, but maybe even more about scaling the organization itself – something that will be discussed in the next section of this chapter. Here we can make the comparison between monolithic systems and microservices: the principles are very much the same. It's incredibly hard to scale a monolithic enterprise that is completely and rigorously governed from the top-down. It's must easier to scale with micro-enterprises with self-governing teams – shift-left! – that can concentrate on specific tasks and operate closely to the customer. This is exactly what the concept of micro-enterprises does and what we already discussed as the principle of unbundling and rebundling.

Once again, compare it to systems. Upgrading a monolithic system is hard and risky. You would likely have to take down the entire system, upgrade every single component, and then bring it back online. It will take a lot of time. Upgrading systems that are composed of microservices will only require the upgrade of a specific service, leaving the rest untouched. We would need to test everything after a service has been upgraded to see if the whole system still works, but there's no need to take the whole system offline – if set up properly. It's the same with enterprises.

Revisiting the Micro-enterprises

We transform the monolithic organizations into an ecosystem of many micro-enterprises who are dynamically interconnected through contracts. These micro-enterprises are not managed top-down but completely customer-driven. Investments in the micro-enterprises are directly related to bringing value to the customer. Above all, these micro-enterprises are fully scalable.

Boundaryless.io presents the entrepreneurial ecosystem enabling organizations, or 3EO. The concept is focused on scaling.

The heart of the model is the micro-enterprise itself, but they come in two flavors: the user micro-enterprise and the node micro-enterprise. The user micro-enterprise is customer-facing, while the node micro-enterprise is a service provider to other micro-enterprises. Both flavors are independent units, holding responsibility for profit and loss. They are entitled to make their own decisions, for instance, in hiring staff.

However, there are services that can be shared among the micro-enterprises. Think of legal counsels or IT systems that are used across the enterprise. These services are provided by a shared service platform. Having these services implemented in each single micro-enterprise will only cause overhead and if fact make the enterprise less scalable. We can compare this with the microservices architecture as well, where so-called sidecars provide generic services to which each microservice has to comply with. Think of security policies that apply to every workload. The microservice contains the functional workload; the sidecar – nonfunctional – ensures that the workload is compliant with security policies.

Next to the shared services platform, micro-enterprises are encouraged to use the same platforms as other micro-enterprises. This is driven by architecture and architecture principles to ensure consistency throughout the entire enterprise. In digital transformation this will likely be a technical platform to land the services of the micro-enterprise. Examples are public clouds as technical platforms.

A logical question that will come up is, aren't these micro-enterprises becoming siloes on their own? No, since micro-enterprises will be part of an ecosystem microcommunity contract (EMC). The EMC will issue a contract that states the shared ambition and goals, based on user scenarios. These user scenarios are the translation of the Voice of the Customer, matching the demands of the customers to the portfolio and capabilities of the enterprise. The EMC will "invite" micro-enterprises to bid on the requested customer demand by proposing how the micro-enterprise can add value to that customer. The EMC couples the micro-enterprises in order to realize the solution, as a collaboration between the micro-enterprises, as shown in Figure 5-1. Once the solution has been developed and deployed, the EMC releases the micro-enterprises and move on to the next cycle.

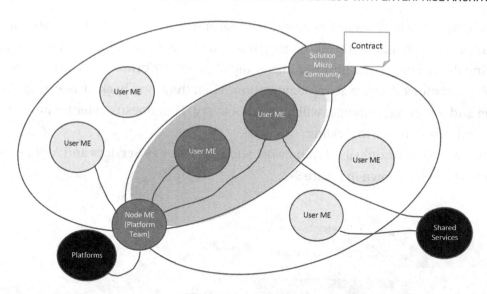

Figure 5-1. *The micro-enterprises model according to Boundaryless.io*

The model is extremely scalable, but micro-enterprises and ecosystems require management too. In fact, it requires supply chain management. All parts of the organization and its ecosystem need to work together to achieve goals and eventually scale. In the next question, we will explore how supply chain management can help with this.

Scaling the Organization: Where to Start

The enterprise architect starts by looking at the entire supply chain and that begins with looking from the business perspective. When an architect mentions supply chain management, this is typically referring to software that is supporting the supply chain. But supply chain management implies so much more. Software is required to support it, but it starts with mastering the supply chain processes. One crucial process in supply chain management is planning. We will discuss this with referral to a study by Hartmut Stadtler of the University of Hamburg, but first we must understand how to embed scaling in the architecture.

Once more, scaling starts with looking from the business perspective and thus we need enterprise architecture. The biggest mistake an enterprise can make is thinking of scaling in terms of technology. Obviously, technology has to enable scaling the business – software and infrastructure – but that doesn't make a business scalable. It's about the entire organization of the enterprise.

161

The enterprise architecture enables business and IT to reach informed decisions on change. That change is directly coming from customer demand. Customer demand is driving the change of the business, including digital transformation. The issue is that a lot of EA frameworks stop at implementation. Then they loop back to assessing the change and the impact changes will have on delivery. That doesn't cater for business agility and certainly not for scaling.

Let's take a commonly used framework such as ITSA – IT Services and Architecture – as an example. It's shown in Figure 5-2.

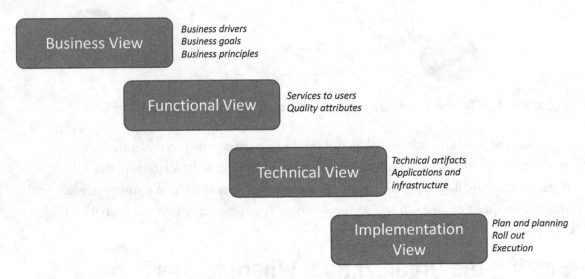

Figure 5-2. *The Original ITSA (IT Services and Architecture) framework*

From the business view, it drills down to the implementation. But architecture doesn't stop there. Modern enterprises should add two more views to this model:

- Innovation view

- Scaling view

But why? Because it's where any business will find the real challenges. In this modern world, the only thing that is a constant is change. The consequence of that is businesses are not executing architecture as a single, straightforward drill down to the actual implementation. There will likely be many implementations and implementations that change along the way due to changing customer demands. If it fails in changing course in time, it will soon be irrelevant to customers. In other words, the digitally transformed enterprise will always be in a beta state. Parallel to implementations done by one team, it needs teams that constantly look at the market, capturing the voice of the customer, and think about innovations. These teams must not only be close to the customer, but also close to the implementation teams.

You can't change course of a ship by just steering at the front, the back side of the ship needs to come along too. The guys controlling the engines need to know whether they need to give the ship more power or less. The navigator on the bridge has to issue clear commands: that's what the architect does.

The scaling view is necessary because of something that we will address in the last section of this chapter: the subscription economy. Anything that is implemented must be scalable: up and down.

The model will start looking like Figure 5-3.

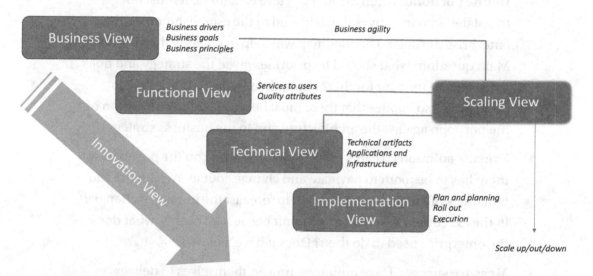

Figure 5-3.   *The adapted ITSA framework with innovation and scaling view*

The business perspective is the starting point. To quote Rick Kash and David Calhoun in *How Companies Win*, "No organization can win if its parts are not all aligned to execute the same strategy and achieve the same goals. Even the 'perfect' strategy within a competitively advantaged business model will ultimately fail if the organization is not fully aligned internally and does not understand how to execute the strategy, or if it works at cross-purposes."

All parts need to be aligned in executing the same strategy and achieve the same goals. That is what business architecture does: it bridges between the business strategy and the execution of that strategy. In a digital transformation, this typically means that the business strategy must match the strategy for implementing and utilizing digital technology, such as cloud and cloud native. For the latter we also need to define a strategy and a roadmap that matches the various stages in executing the business strategy. It has to answer some critical questions during five stages. Whynde Kuehn describes the stages in her book *Strategy to Reality*:

- **Develop strategy**: Is the enterprise business strategy aligned with the technology strategy? How can new business models be fulfilled with technology and how would the roadmap look like?

- **Define architecture**: Business and technology strategy must be integrated in the overarching business and enterprise strategy.

- **Define portfolio**: When the architecture is defined, it must be translated into initiatives that will lead to the establishment of the enterprise portfolio. The roadmap will help in creating this portfolio. Main question: What should be priorities given the strategy and does the architecture cater for that? If not, then we need to take a step back. This also implies that there must be a continuous validation of the portfolio against the architecture and to the business strategy.

- **Execute solutions**: Teams create solutions based on the portfolio, but there has to be room to navigate and change course. We can use the outcomes of the scenario planning to forecast the impact of changes in the execution. When priorities shift because of events, what does the enterprise need to do then? Does it have a plan B?

- **Measure success**: Have initiatives proven themselves to deliver the expected added value to the customer, and with that, are they fulfilling the business strategy?

Now we have to map the organization to the strategy. We want the adaptive, flexible, and scalable organization. Most enterprises will look at SAFe to do this, since SAFe has become the standard for working at scale. But implementing SAFe is a lot of work and takes a lot of effort. Implementing SAFe in the wrong way can kill a business.

SAFe enables business agility: the domains in SAFe correspond with the stages that Kuehn describes. SAFe promotes the following:

- Lean–agile leadership, actively promoting and leading change through the enterprise.

- Continuous learning culture, fostering the growth mindset and challenging creativity.

- Lean portfolio management, aligning strategy with execution, aiming to optimize operations – remember that lean ops is a must to free up staff to stimulate innovation. Operations and innovations go hand in hand.

- Organizational agility to enable fast responses to opportunities and threats to the business.

- Team and technical agility, wherein business and technical teams work together on business solutions.

- Agile product delivery, focusing on the customer as the "center of product strategy," developing products to fulfill customer demand by applying continuous innovation, integration, and deployment of new products or new releases of that product.

- Enterprise solution delivery, coordinating and aligning the entire supply chain through continuous evaluation of systems.

The problem with SAFe is that either you implement it in the enterprise, or you don't. There's no in-between model for this. Remember: All parts of the enterprise must be aligned. You can't have one part of the organization working in SAFe and another part is working in a different governance model. We can make this very tangible with an example.

From the strategic themes, epics have been defined. That is translated into products that must be delivered by various teams. Products are next detailed in product breakdown items that are listed in the backlog for the teams. There will be several teams, several backlogs, and a multitude of product items that must be delivered. At the end, it all needs to come together in fulfilling strategic epics. But what typically happens is this:

The strategy is defined. The portfolio is defined. Teams are assembled. Kanban boards are filled. In theory every team knows exactly what to do.

The software development team starts working on code. It runs the code through pipelines and at the end of the sprint they're ready to deploy. But we are in a corporate environment with corporate rules. The enterprise has a CISO that has defined a process for releasing a new version of software to production. One rule in that process is that this security team must assess the firewall rules before deployment. That is not automated, and it's certainly not included in the pipelines. It's a form that must be manually filled out. Assessment takes two weeks, since it must be planned for the next sprint.

Not realistic? On the contrary, this happens a lot. That's why the entire enterprise needs to work in the same model. To stick with the ship analogy and the "floating architecture," you can't have multiple steering wheels on the same ship. You can have more engines, but they need to operate in sync. Only when all parts are in sync, we can achieve business agility.

Applying the Rules of Supply Chain Management

If we don't have all parts operating in sync, there's also no way that we can scale the business. We have discussed that scaling can only be successful when all parts scale. With SAFe we still have not ensured that all parts are aligned in achieving the strategy. We need something else: the principles of supply chain management.

Now we come at the study by Hartmut Stadtler of the University of Hamburg (refer to `http://196.190.117.157:8080/jspui/bitstream/123456789/23567/1/45%202008.pdf#page=25`). He defines two views on supply chain and these views make it very clear how supply chain influence business agility and scaling. The first view is a broad one where he states that supply chain consists of two or more separated organizations. These organizations – enterprises – can be linked through material flows, data flows, and financial flows. They have a shared goal, though. The enterprises will be delivering products and services to an end customer. So, they are mostly linked through the customer.

Then there's a narrow view. In this case we have a single, large enterprise that might be operating from different sites. The principle is still the same: the enterprise needs to coordinate materials, data, and finances flowing through different sites and enterprise divisions. In theory, Stadtler claims decision-making should be easier since it's one organization with a "single top management level." This is only valid though if all parts and components of the enterprise share the same vision, goals, and ambition, embraced in the EA.

Stadtler now introduces the term "competitiveness." The objective of supply chain management should be increasing competitiveness, since not a single division of the enterprise – or in the broader view, the enterprise as a whole – will be solely responsible for the competitiveness of the end products and services that are delivered to the customer. To put it differently, the customer doesn't experience the outcome of one, single entity, but the results of collaboration in the supply chain. The competition has shifted from single enterprises to these chains. And then Stadtler draws an interesting conclusion: "Obviously, to convince an individual company to become a part of a supply chain requires a win-win situation for each participant in the long run." We can now add to that: that win-win situation will only be achieved if all participants understand that they are part of a chain that must be entirely scalable, addressing customer needs as the entire chain.

We must align all parts in the enterprise and its ecosystem. In accordance with the House of Quality that was discussed in Chapter 3, Stadtler talks about the House of Supply Chain Management (SCM). The model is shown in Figure 5-4.

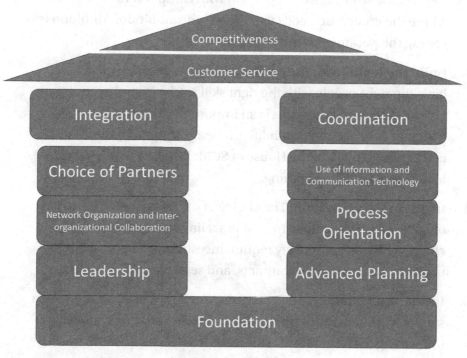

Figure 5-4. *The House of SCM*

Competitiveness is defined by customer service: How well is the customer serviced? That service and moreover the experience of that service is defined by two pillars in the House of SCM: integration and coordination. It takes leadership to make the right choices in who must be integrated parts of the chain and how these parts collaborate. The collaboration itself is depending on the coordination, which is in essence the way *how* parts connect, share information, and agree on the joint plans and planning. The foundation layer is all about tools and eventually technology enabling the activities in the two pillars.

The House of SCM can be recognized in every step a business has to take in order to scale. These steps are as follows:

1. **Understand your customer**: Capture the Voice of the Customer. It all starts with these basic questions: Who is the customer, why and when are they buying, how do they perceive your enterprise, what are they expecting?

2. **Asses the competition**: This starts with self-reflection – how is the enterprise doing in comparison with competitors? It defines where the enterprise needs to go, it sets the ambition. Ambition is setting the parameters and the need for scale.

3. **Build the teams with the right skills**: The enterprise must have the right people with the right skill set. This might require investments, and again, this is an important driver for the business case and the capabilities to scale. It's part of the coordination pillar in the House of SCM. Building teams requires a plan and accurate planning.

4. **Invest in the ecosystem**: The choice of partners in the House of SCM. Who do we need to enable scaling in the entire supply chain? This will definitely require investments in partnerships, understandings, supply contracts, and service-level agreements.

5. **Invest in technology**: The enterprise must be in a permanent beta state, continuously listening to the customer and continuously innovating to stay relevant. This leads to a lean operation, freeing up skilled staff to work on new products and services, shifting to development. Lean operations are achieved by automation, reducing toil in operations. But we also need technology to integrate and coordinate in the supply chain. And to start with, we need technology to capture the Voice of the Customer, for instance, Customer Relationship Management (CRM) systems. Lastly, we need technology to manage our business and architecture. But keep in mind, technology is an enabler, nothing more. It's not a driver for digital transformation: the voice of the customer is the driver for digital transformation.

6. **Mature the processes**: Processes often start in an "ad hoc" modus. Mature processes are repeatable and have predictable outcomes. Processes must be well defined, documented, and brought under change control.

7. **Automate the processes**: Repeatable processes with predictable processes can be automated. Automation will reduce manual intervention and is less prone to errors and more important less extensive in labor and associated costs. Costs that are saved can be invested again in development. A common misunderstanding or misperception is that automation will kill jobs. On the contrary, it creates jobs – more interesting jobs.

8. **Get sales in place**: Scaling can be both up and down, but off course we are getting our enterprise ready for expanding the business, thus scaling up. That doesn't happen by magic: we need sales and a sales strategy. Who are we targeting? Do we understand what the customer wants? What are the best sales channels? Most important, can we deliver – at scale?

9. **Get cutting-edge marketing**: Remarkably enough, marketing is the first discipline that gets cut when times get rough. That's business suicide. Without marketing, there's no reason to have scaling processes in place. In its very core, scaling is about developing once and sell and deploy many times. So, we are scaling sales, innovation, and (automated) operations. Marketing has to scale too: it continuously must scan the market for new trends and identify opportunities to allow the business to stay beta.

10. **Avoid the most common pitfalls**:

    - Hesitate to recruit staff with the right skills.

    - Mistaking scaling with growth.

    - Thinking that scaling is only one way up... and not down too.

    - Forcing scaling without a proper business case.

    - Working from a monolithic business and enterprise architecture.

- Scaling without having processes and technology in place as the foundation.

- Selling without having supply chain and delivery in place – this will kill any effort in landing and expanding any business.

To summarize how to start scaling the business:

- **Assess and plan, think in scenarios**: Start with a forecast, including amount of customers, orders, and the ambition in terms of revenue and profit. That will define the business case. Apply the scenarios according to the scenario planning that we discussed in the first section of this chapter. What happens if we sell more or less? What happens if we add staff and systems? How does it impact the business? Be aware that scaling will require investments. Costs will go up. Do exactly the same thing for decreasing business: what is the impact? Can we scale down without hampering the core activities of the enterprise and still be agile enough to change course?

- **Think in ecosystems**: No division is on its own, no enterprise is on its own. Think from the principles of supply chain management and the House of SCM. If our enterprise scales, the entire chain must scale with it. That takes leadership, coordination, and integration. Be aware of the weak spots in the chain and fix these with priority before further scaling. Be hard on yourself in recognizing weak spots. Denial is futile.

There's still one question that we must answer to conclude this chapter. At the beginning of this chapter, we stated that businesses need to be scalable, and we sort of touched the reasons why they must be scalable. There's one market trend that makes business agility and scalability even critical, causing big enterprises to fail if they don't adopt the new rules of this era.

Let's talk about the subscription era.

A New Business Era: Everything As Subscription

The term subscription economy was invented by Tien Tzuo of Zuora. He identifies the shift that companies make to relationships with customers. Enterprises don't build a relationship by a one-off sell of a product, but with subscriptions, creating loyalty of customers to the enterprise. But subscriptions come with challenges, especially in architecture. Just think of the characteristics of a subscription. Customers can do a lot with subscriptions that they can't do by just buying a product.

Customers can

- Submit

- Change

- Pause

- Reinitiate

- Stop

a subscription. That's exactly the reason why scalability is likely one of the most important quality attributes in architecture.

In a sense, the customer is making the same shift as companies. Most companies are shifting from CAPEX to OPEX, from capital expenditure to operational expenditure. With CAPEX, companies purchase assets as investments, written off over a fixed period of time, regardless if the asset is used or not. It's paid for and will depreciate over time.

With OPEX the company only pays for the day-to-day usage to operate the business. It's the reason why enterprises are moving assets to public clouds, where it doesn't have to buy servers, network equipment, and other devices, but pay for services they actually use to run the business. In fact, cloud is one big subscription. The rationale for an enterprise to do this: business agility and scalability... up and down. Pay what you use. If services are stopped, the company doesn't pay for it any longer. And they don't have to pay for hardware, since it isn't property of the enterprise. The hardware belongs to the cloud provider; the enterprise only "hires" space on that hardware for as long as they need it.

Customers are going through the exact same cycle. They shift from purchasing and owning stuff to merely hiring it as long as they need it. They only pay for the time they use it. This requires scaling: a company being able to deliver services "on demand," in shape, form, and time. That defines the experience of the customer, including profiting from upgrades and innovations.

Customers pay for the experience. Mastering scaling is essential to that customer experience.

Summary

If there's one lesson you have to remember from this chapter, it's that scaling can be both ways. Businesses must be able to scale up, but also down if circumstances force an enterprise to decrease production. Scaling is not synonym to growth. Growth will lead to scaling, but an enterprise must be ready and prepared to scale down as well and still be able to operate a profitable business.

We studied why scaling is important to business agility and how we organize our enterprise to enable scaling. Scaling is depending on proper functioning of chains. A chain is as strong as its weakest link; therefore, scaling is very much depending on aligning and synchronization all parts in that chain, within the enterprise, and in its ecosystem. The disconnection in the chain is often the reason why scaling fails.

We've learned that the principles of supply chain management can help us in scaling business. But it all starts with assess and plan, thinking in scenarios and forecasting. Next, the enterprise and especially the enterprise architect must think in terms of ecosystems. No enterprise is an entity on itself in this connected, digitally transformed world.

We also learned that scaling is about capacity and capabilities. Architects tend to think in terms of systems, but the human factor is as equally important. We need people with the right skills and mindset. The classic roles will probably not be sufficient any longer to keep the enterprise on the ever-changing digital track. Roles are changing. People will be continuously learning, one of the pillars in the SAFe framework. In the final chapter of this book, we will discuss these changing roles.

CHAPTER 6

The Changing Role of the Enterprise Architect

Enterprises are changing due to digital transformation and so is the role of the enterprise architect (EA). In this final chapter we will discuss how this role is changing and what the key capabilities must be of the modern EA. We will study how the role of the EA was originally defined in EA frameworks such as TOGAF and next discover how this role is shifting with the introduction and implementation of agile working and DevSecOps. Maybe even more important, the EA still needs to have deep knowledge of business processes and technology, but the modern EA also has to develop his soft skills, also known as power or life skills. The modern EA is firstly a communicator.

The Role of the Architect in Frameworks

Let's start by identifying what the enterprise architect was and what their tasks were. The role of the EA has been described in full details in a variety of frameworks. Some of the role descriptions are listed in the following texts. Spoiler alert: You will notice that there are quite some differences in these descriptions.

Let's first explore what TOGAF thinks an enterprise architect is. "A major task of the Enterprise Architect is to communicate complex technical information to all stakeholders of the project, including those who do not have a technical background. Strong negotiation and problem-solving skills are also required."

So, apparently the EA has a ton of technical knowledge and they are able to translate that knowledge into language that can be understood by persons who are not technically skilled. Next, the EA must have the skills to convince every single stakeholder that a specific technical solution is the best way forward in a project. It's the only thing that TOGAF says about the enterprise architect itself – which is something different than describing enterprise architecture as the domain.

© Jeroen Mulder 2023

J. Mulder, *Modern Enterprise Architecture*, https://doi.org/10.1007/978-1-4842-9066-8_6

However, the role description is very limited, only mentioning the technical skills. By now, after reading the previous five chapters, you probably understood that the EA does a lot more and tasks are not restricted by knowledge about technology. The technical knowledge is important, but not the most important aspect of the role.

Remarkable enough, defining technology is not the aim of TOGAF. The frameworks seek to be a guidance for the design of business architecture, supported by architecture for technical infrastructure. Next, it describes how enterprises can implement and organize governance, including change management which is an important aspect in the framework. The basic idea of that is that enterprises will always be subject to change, where TOGAF expects these changes to come from the business. The Architecture Development Method (ADM) cycle starts with the business for that reason. On the other hand, requirements management sits in the heart of the cycle. Every phase in the cycle, including defining architecture for data, applications, and infrastructure, is driven by requirements management. Hence, the assumption is that, for instance, infrastructure can have requirements on its own, not coming from business requirements or business-initiated changes.

The strength of TOGAF is that it enables decoupling between different layers of architecture. As we have discussed in the previous chapters, modern architectures will be driven by the principles of microservices and the service-oriented architecture (SOA). These architectures are modular and very scalable, which is important for the modern enterprise as we have concluded in Chapter 5. In SOA and microservices architecture, services are decoupled from underlying infrastructure, including compute instances, network, and operating systems. But these architectures also come with a challenge and that is interoperability. Services must be able to discover each other and know how to communicate with other services. In SOA and microservices, the usage of standard APIs – or application programming interfaces – has become crucial. But if defined, designed, and implemented well, these architectures ensure modularity, flexibility, and reusability of components.

The big question is, is SOA and designing for microservices technology or architecture? Both offer a lot of advantages for businesses: flexibility, modularity, and with that scalability being among these advantages. But without a single doubt, an architect will need technological knowledge to create solutions based on the principles of SOA and microservices.

TOGAF is underlining the value add that technology must have to businesses. For that reason, TOGAF is still very much focusing on the technical part of the role that the EA has. Still, it would make more sense to have a broader description of the role of the EA.

Let's have a look at other EA frameworks and how they perceive the role of the enterprise architect. Zachman sees the EA more as a doctor. He has knowledge of the human body, knows how to set a diagnosis, and next, is able to define a solution. The diagnosis – the definition of the business problem in this metaphor – is supported by models, such as scans that represent parts of the body. Hence, the doctor also has to understand how he must read and interpret the models. But in Zachman's view these models are only a toolkit. The main task of the EA is to set the diagnosis and to come up with a good prescription for a solution. Although technology is an important asset in Zachman, there's more focus on organizing and planning the architecture. Zachman even calls this "planner," capturing business data, processes, events, and business motivation. From there Zachman drills down to data models that drive the business architecture. Technology is merely supporting.

Gartner recently released reports and white papers where they indicate the new role of the EA. In their view the EA is the main driver for digital transformation of the enterprise. Gartner underlines the technology aspects of the job: the EA being responsible for a data-driven and event-driven architecture that is powered by cloud and cloud-native technology. But, also Gartner acknowledges the shift that EA makes from IT to business. The EA will be working more closely with the business stakeholders and evolve to "internal management consultancy" supporting digital strategy and technological innovation.

Finally, SAFe – the Scaled Agile Framework (© Scaled Agile, Inc.) – also holds a definition of the enterprise architect. "The Enterprise Architect establishes a technology strategy and roadmap that enables a portfolio to support current and future business capabilities. They drive design, engineering, reuse, application of patterns, and create Enabler Epics for the architectures that comprise the solutions in a portfolio."

This short definition is already a lot broader than TOGAF, and it – important – mentions that the EA supports business capabilities. SAFe also includes responsibilities for the EA. The most important ones:

- Collaborating with portfolio management to "provide a high-level vision of enterprise solutions and development initiatives." In this book we called this the North Star: the reflection of the ambition of the business, followed by the development of a roadmap that contain the building blocks to achieve that ambition.

- Understanding and communicating the strategy of the business and the forthcoming drivers for architecture. The EA is responsible for communicating these drivers to solution architects and other stakeholders.

- Driving initiatives for building and improving architecture, including collecting and generating innovative ideas that will help the business moving forward.

- Promoting continuous delivery pipeline and DevOps capabilities. We are adding Site Reliability Engineering to this.

- Promoting the reuse of architectural artifacts, including gcode, components, and patterns.

In SAFe, the EA really drives the business. How? By capturing the Voice of the Customer and through collaboration within the enterprise and across the enterprise ecosystem using agile techniques and DevSecOps with continuous delivery pipelines.

The choice of technology is important and a prioritized task for the EA. But as we have learned in this book, the chosen technology must enable agile working and responding to customer demand fast. The modern EA must have knowledge about cloud-native technologies and architectural concepts such as microservices, service mesh, event- and data-driven architectures, and integration of PaaS and SaaS solutions. The EA has to work together with other architects and engineers to implement these technologies, making sure they add value to the business.

- Solution architects

- Cloud architects

- DevOps engineers

But the EA also needs to work with the business.

- Business analysts

- Financial analysts

- Business managers

If the EA has to work with all these different roles, where does the EA sit in the organization? To justify the overarching view and enable mandate in driving the overall business from technology, the EA should be high ranked, reporting to the C level. There's however a risk in giving the EA this position. He might end up in an ivory tower.

We want our modern EA working with the teams, as a servant leader.

From Architect to Servant Leader

It's good to start with a definition of the servant leader before we move on.

A servant leader is someone who aims to help other people and their organization grow. By being servant to others and the organization, the leader will experience growth him- or herself. This way of leadership comes with specific soft skills, which are more important than the technical skills of the EA. Technical skills can be studied and learned, where soft, personal skills are something that must be cultivated to grow. Think of

- Being a listener

- Being empathic

- Being able to build and maintain relationships

- Being committed to the growth of other people

- Being able to build communities

- Being able to reflect on yourself

- Being able to develop and share a vision

- Being able to influence

Now, let's look at the role of the architect. We start at looking at the traditional role of the architect.

The term architect has led to many debates. What is an architect, to begin with? In many companies, the architect is an IT guy. It's the person who designs technical solutions for businesses. The architect defines the guidelines for the software that is used, how networks and other infrastructure components are implemented. The architect also monitors if and how security guardrails are applied across all IT components. The designs and plans are executed by teams of specialists, managed by a project lead. The team might consist of network engineers, infrastructure specialists, software engineers, database administrators, and other subject matter experts. They all execute parts of the architecture.

That's only the build phase. After the environment has been set up, it's handed over to the operations. Again, the operations team will have various experts in the different domains. This is the typical model that is used in offshoring. The network is looked after by network administrators, the databases are managed by database administrators, the underlying storage is the domain of the storage specialist, and so on. There will even be separate database specialists for SQL and NoSQL, or even specific database environments such as IBM DB2 or Oracle. The architecture is the guidebook, where the architect is supposed to oversee it all.

Changes are validated against the architecture before they are carried out. There's often a list of small changes such as updates, but major changes are always verified with the architect – who checks with the subject matter experts what the impact might be of a specific change. The architect in many cases has the final say.

That's the old world. It's a completely siloed world with a big wall between development and operations. Is the architect a servant leader here? They might have some of the servant skills, but their role is not servant. The architect sets the scene and controls it. They're the chief with the overview.

In cloud this already works completely different. An architect in the cloud is in many cases someone who actually sits behind the wheel and might even build stuff. If we want to get a good understanding of what a cloud architect does, we only have to look at the certifications for an architect in, for example, Microsoft Azure.

The certification path for Azure Architect starts with the fundamentals in AZ-900, which basically teaches what cloud and specifically Azure is. Then the real work starts with the AZ-104, where you will learn to implement and manage storage, compute resources, and network components in Azure. The Azure architect can do it all, including hands-on work. This is actually an administrator certificate, but it is a prerequisite to go into the next level: the solution architect. Skills that will be tested:

- Design identity, governance, and monitoring solutions

- Design data storage solutions

- Design business continuity solutions

- Design infrastructure solutions

The exams contain labs to prove that the architect can really build this in Azure. AWS and Google Cloud follow the same approach to upskill architects.

But that's not enterprise architecture. True. And not true. If we define the EA as the person that works on IT on an enterprise level – thus for the entire company – then we're already getting close with the skills of the cloud architect. But, the primary role of the EA is to connect IT with the business, as we have learned from the discussed EA frameworks. Right, but every cloud architect will only build stuff in cloud that will benefit the business in the first place, based on business requirements. Cloud for the sake of cloud doesn't make any sense at all.

The key is that the cloud architect is multiskilled and comes close to being an EA. They are able to translate business requirements into solutions, and they can design and build these solutions. They have knowledge of all the required components in cloud, including compute, storage, and network. They are able to connect to application architects and software developers; they can connect business with IT and work with all stakeholders in the enterprise.

This will require at least a set of the skills that we defined at the beginning of this section.

Establishing the Servant Leader Role

We are getting to the servant leader part. The architect has technical knowledge, but more importantly is aiming to help their team – and with that the business – grow.

The team often used to look like Figure 6-1.

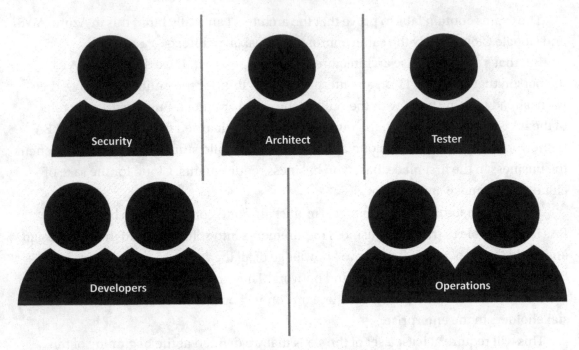

Figure 6-1. *The organization in teams in the traditional enterprise*

A major step forward is to bring all these roles together in one team, as a first step to create DevOps teams (Figure 6-2).

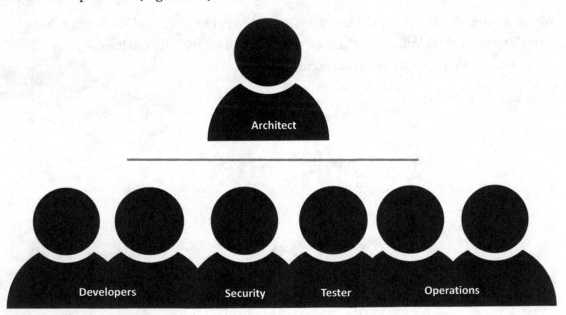

Figure 6-2. *Creating DevOps teams*

The problem here is that the team is likely not mandated to take decisions. The architect is still "floating" above the team, not really being part of the team. All members of the team have their specialties and will work together to deliver the products and services, according to instructions that they get from the architect. But there's probably no continuous communication. Decisions will have to wait for the verdict of the architect and basically slow down the entire process.

We can change that by giving the architect the role of the servant leader (Figure 6-3).

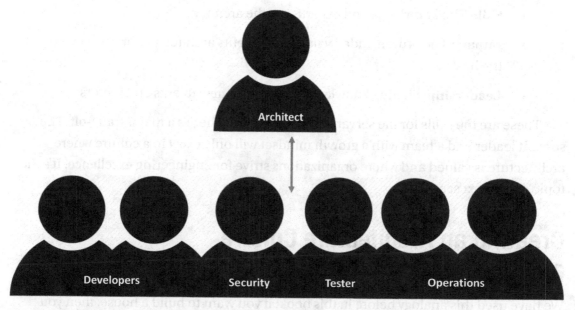

Figure 6-3. *The architect as servant leader, part of the team*

There's regular communication with the architect, enabling the team to make timely decisions. The architect attends the daily stand-up meetings, so that issues or ideas for improvement can be immediately discussed. The architect as the servant leader stimulates the creation of new ideas, improving the products. They're not managing the team, they're supporting the team in making the right choices and decisions. This team is supported by the servant leader, a peer among peers.

But who's the architect in this case? Are we expecting the EA to be the peer among peers? Or is the EA still more of the strategist? Or both?

If we must draw one conclusion, then it's that the IT, cloud, or enterprise architect doesn't exist. Gregor Hohpe recognizes different types of architects in his book *The Software Architect Elevator*. What is an enterprise architect in the view of Hohpe? Referring to literature, he defines the EA as the linking pin between business and technology. But, "Only if the two are well aligned does IT provide value to the business," appreciating the fact that business and IT are not always on the same planet. Said in different wording, IT is from Mars and business from Venus. This makes it hard by default for the EA to connect business with IT. Yet, it's the number one job of the EA.

Hohpe also defines the key capabilities for an architect, something he refers to as the three-legged stool – since a three-legged stool doesn't wobble. It's as stable as anything, you can't push it over. The three legs are as follows:

- **Skill**: The knowledge and expertise of the architect

- **Impact**: The proven added value and benefits architecture brings to the business

- **Leadership**: Sharing knowledge, mentoring new talents and juniors

These are the skills for the servant leader. However, there's a major trade-off. The servant leader and a team with a growth mindset will only excel in a culture where architecture is valued and where organizations strive for engineering excellence. It's the topic of the next section.

Creating an Architecture Culture and Engineering Excellence

We have used this analogy before in this book: if you want to build a house, then you need to think about how the house will look like and, next, define the foundation on which the house will stand. There's no point in laying out the foundation first and then start thinking about the house. This logical way of thinking is one of the cornerstones of architecture. Enterprises and enterprise architects call this "working with or under architecture."

Architecture in a sense isn't anything else than making sure that whenever the enterprise develops, builds, and manages a product or a service, it makes sure that these products and services adhere to foundational principles and standards that all stakeholders have agreed upon. This applies to every process in an enterprise, including IT. Architecture helps organizations to get a grip on business operations and IT systems that enable these business operations. Business goals, strategy, and ambition – our North Star – are always leading in architecture. IT should support these goals and ambition – not the other way around, meaning that IT is never a goal on itself, not even in digital transformation. We're only using cloud and cloud native to enhance our business.

Working with architecture can add a lot of value for organizations and also save costs. However, this is not always the case. Support within the organization, leadership, vision, and a shared sense of urgency are important success factors.

In other words, the path to the North Star and the strategy for digital transformation must be clear and supported by every stakeholder. The arguments for the transformation must be rational.

There's a good example that explains how important it is to have the debate on digital transformation and using cloud technology with the right arguments. The example is coming from the Dutch government "allowing departments" to start using public cloud services. The argument used: it's probably cheaper. That's not the right argument to start with. The argument should be: delivering better services to our citizens through faster innovations, less downtime when we're doing updates and upgrades, less need for heavy operations through automation so that we can have our expensive people working on these innovations instead of fixing toil.

Cheaper? In public services, we're talking about sensitive data of citizens. Hence, security is priority number one. The public cloud platforms AWS, Azure, and so forth are likely the best-protected platforms in the world. They have to with millions of customers on their systems. But, they are responsible of the cloud; the customer is responsible of what's in the cloud. Cloud providers offer great toolboxes to protect data, but it's up to the customer to use these tools. These tools come at a cost, but security is not a menu where you can pick and choose from. Either you have security fully in place or you don't.

These are the debates where the EA must step in and make sure that the right arguments come to the table. The right arguments are the ones that underline the business value add. The truth is that an EA that is perceived to be more technical than business strategic will find it hard to bring business arguments to the debate. That's the heritage of EA being seen as mainly IT focused. IT, on itself, is still very often seen as a cost or service center and not as the business enabler. Let alone, IT as the driver for business innovation, fulfilling even long-term business strategies. Enterprises who are dealing with digital transformation are transforming into companies where IT is no longer just a service department, but a crucial enabler of the digital, data-driven, and event-driven business. Business and IT now really must align not only to support each other but also to operate as joint forces to grow the business. That means that the enterprise must start working under architecture.

We're not coming from an easy place in most enterprises. Over the years, the IT landscape will have grown dramatically leaving us with technical debt, including many applications, data sprawl, and on top of it all, a lot of processes. Costs of managing these environments will probably have gone through the roof, leading to massive cost-cutting programs, and a variety of outsource and outtasking plans, leading to even more processes to keep (functional) control over the landscape and the multitude of suppliers. It all ended up on the plate of the EA, who we are now asking to lead and drive digital transformation to enhance business.

How can modern enterprise architecture help to solve this chaos? By looking at architecture in a different way. Not as the technical solution, but as the strategic, organizational solution. Architecture is above all a management tool to support the professionalization of organizations and to coordinate the coherence of process architecture, business architecture, application architecture, and technical architecture.

We need different types of architecture, not only focusing on the technical aspects, but on many different business components and how these components are linked with each other. In other words, there's not one sort of architecture. Architecture consists of many domains, and in the right architecture culture, these domains work seamlessly together. What are these domains?

- Enterprise architecture

- Solution architecture

- Domain architecture

- Application architecture

- Infrastructure architecture

All these components are depending on each other; in the end, they form a chain. You can't simply add technology without impacting that chain. If we want to add technology, we need an overview of all dependencies in that chain. But even more important and something that we have stressed in this book, we need to have an answer on the question why the business would need specific technology. What is the business added value? A crucial role that the EA has is to embed architecture in the organization, on all layers, and in all domains. Architecture processes must be in place and the right architecture roles assigned with the appropriate responsibilities and corresponding mandates. Architecture frameworks are a good guidance.

Enterprises should not make the mistake to leverage IT architecture into that role. The enterprise will only cover for the technical part of the architecture. The enterprise that is evolving into the digital transformation will have to make serious investments in architecture. That is a transformation in itself. There will be developers and administrators but also business owners who will feel that they are restricted in their work if the enterprise adopts the principles of EA, setting guidelines and guardrails for all enterprise components. We are doing this for the entire company: that should be the message to all stakeholders involved.

EA will offer great benefits to every organization, simply by providing a clear structure, well-defined processes, and guidance in implementing changes in the various domains of the enterprise. Start working from the current situation and assess what architecture could bring in achieving the enterprise goals. What is the desired situation? Where does the enterprise want to be in given amount of time? Architecture will prevent teams from just doing things but will provide clear guardrails in how to do things so that efforts result in the desired – and expected – outcomes. We will start working from IST to SOLL, from a current mode to a future mode, yet guided by conventions of architecture.

We are building an architect mindset across the enterprise. It means that we must educate all stakeholders in the importance of EA and show how changes in the architectural change will impact the business of the enterprise. Every stakeholder, every member of staff must be aware of business impact. If a website is slow and customers aren't able to get orders in or get answers to inquiries, that has a significant impact on the customer satisfaction. In a digital age, negative experiences can cause severe problems to a company. It's not the question if this will impact the business, but how it is impacted and how severe it is. At the end, customers will leave if problems aren't fixed. Changes, new releases, updates, and upgrades must be tested and fully traceable, supported by architecture. Incidents quickly resolved, enabled by clear documentation of the architecture. Just for clarity, documentation is not a synonym for heavyweight, zillion-page documents, but can also be clear, yet extensive metadata in code, centrally stored in a repository.

An architecture mindset also means that developers, engineers, administrators, and basically every other stakeholder communicate with each other. Architecture is communication. Who does what, when, and why? And, have all relevant stakeholders been involved? Communication skills are essential for any architect or person who fulfills an architectural role. We are all in this together.

Indeed, these are the skills of the servant leader.

The final remaining question is, who do we need in the organization to get architecture done in the future, where enterprises are in the midst of the digital transformation, changing their way of working with agile and creating DevSecOps teams? We'll try to explore some ideas on that in the next section.

The Future of Architecture and the Architect

To define the future of the architect, we must first look at the future of architecture itself and how it will evolve over the coming years. EA is the enabler and the accelerator of digital transformation. But EA needs to go through a transformation in itself to become that enabler and accelerator.

First, we must set a strategic direction for EA. This means that in most companies we must leverage EA to become a business-level priority. Next, EA has to include all enterprise components. In digital companies, there will be an emphasis on technology enabling that digital transformation. There's a risk that digital transformation programs will be limited to IT where the transformation will impact the entire business. From an IT perspective, it's easy to build a webshop. What happens if customers shift from a physical store to buying via that webshop? How is the supply chain set up? Who's picking up the orders? How are payments checked? Are payments done on the website itself of through third-party payment apps? What contracts does the enterprise need to service payments through these apps? Be aware that an outage in any of these components in the chain can cause severe losses to the enterprise that has moved its sales to online channels. It's all subject to EA.

EA will be responsible to draw a plan for the enterprise, covering business processes from demand to supply, supported by enabling systems and supporting technology.

But we also need focus, especially in the world of digital. Focus comes with choices. There's a lot to choose from in the digital world. Just as a fun game: google on "periodic table of tools." There are a lot of periodic tables, analogue to the real periodic table of elements, that provide overview of tools in various technology domains. The concept was copied to a table with DevOps tools by XebiaLabs that today is published by Digital.ai (`https://digital.ai/devops-tools-periodic-table`). But the concept is spreading. For good reasons, since it provides a comprehensive method to view different technology solutions in IT and cloud. The best ones are interactive, allow for selection per group, and provide more information per product or service by clicking a tile.

EA has an important role in building a solid foundation and managing a consistent roadmap for technology. The foundation is essential for development teams that develop, test, and deploy new features, products, and services. If the foundation is not solid and the technology stack not consistent with clearly defined patterns, development teams will lose track and might be ending up in building stuff that doesn't "fit" the foundation. Focus on consistency and best practices, and a clear portfolio will accelerate development.

Lastly, EA needs to architect for scaling, the topic of the previous chapter.

Now, let's get to the organization of architecture and the roles that we need to start defining EA. For that, we turn to IT4IT and agile working. Architect Rob Akershoek published a model that might help in answering the question about who we need to guide the digital transformation. The model is shown in Figure 6-4.

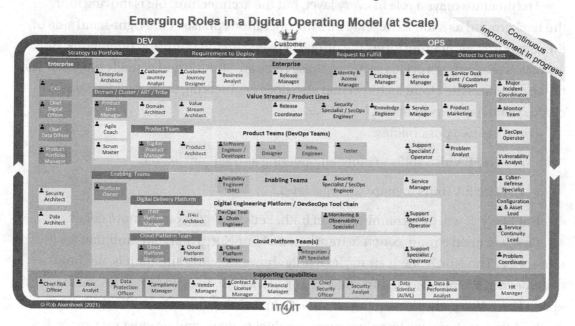

Figure 6-4. *Model for emerging roles in a digital operating model (by courtesy of Rob Akershoek, IT4IT)*

This model makes perfectly clear with who the EA has to cooperate in a scaling organization. Be aware: The model only contains roles, not to be mistaken by persons. One person can have more than one role.

The architecture roles are represented in the yellow boxes. So, we have as a minimal set:

- Enterprise architect

- Domain and value stream architect

- Product architect

- Cloud platform architect

- Security architect

- Data architect

You will undoubtedly recognize many of these roles from earlier sections.

Architecture plays a role in every layer, but the architecture role is moving more to the background as soon as we slide into the operations phase at the right-hand side of the diagram. Engineering forms the bridge between architecture and operations. But as we have seen in the previous sections, these roles are shifting and actually blurring. The best example is the cloud architect that also does engineering work, building assets in cloud. What happens to the EA?

There are two possibilities:

- The EA also shifts to more engineering as a servant leader.

- The EA shifts to more strategic level.

But likely, it will be a combination of both. Let's work this out in more detail.

First, we need a more concrete translation of our North Star: our ambition for the enterprise. The North Star is strategic. It only shows what the ambition is, not how to achieve it. We need something that we can work with. In agile terms this will be epics. The EA already plays an important role in defining the epics, although in agile methodologies there will be epic owners, product owners, and product managers that manage these epics.

What is an epic?

- An epic translates the strategic objectives of the enterprise – the North Star – into deliverables that add value to the enterprise strategy.

- The epic focuses on the value for the customer or end user and on the expected outcome for the enterprise when the value is delivered.

- The epic has to generate significant added value to the business, to be proven through a minimal viable product (MVP).

- Since the epic is formulated on strategic level, it's likely too large for delivery as a whole. Therefore, the epic is divided into smaller artifacts such as products and features. The advantage is that different teams can work on these products and features and contribute to the delivery of the epic.

- An epic requires an epic owner who manages the underlying business case. The epic will almost in every case require significant investments of the enterprise. Products and value streams adding to the epic are managed by product owners and product managers.

- Shaping the epic for future releases is called refinement. This is documented in roadmaps describing iterative steps in realization and improvement of epics, depending on business outcomes. Progress is monitored in reviews of the roadmap.

The epic is the what; the epic roadmap describes the how – compliant with our North Star analogy. The epic roadmap describes how to achieve the goals of the epic.

- The epic roadmap contains a more detailed view of the steps that must be taken to fulfill the epic. It holds a delivery plan and a financial forecast that must be in line with the overall business case for the epic.

- The epic owner creates the epic roadmap together with all relevant stakeholders: portfolio owners, business representatives, business analysts, and various architects. They are consulted on a regular basis, but also when deemed necessary for further detailing of the roadmap.

- The epic roadmap is a document that defines the how, meaning that it describes the deliverables such as products and features. Main drivers to continuously refine the roadmap are business demands and business events (think of mergers and acquisitions), technology trends, and the most important one, the Voice of the Customer.

Now, what is the role of the EA in defining epics and epic roadmaps? Here's where the debate starts. Organizations that implement agile working in full will probably assign epic owners. The main tasks of the epic owner being:

- The epic owner is the interface between all stakeholders in delivering the products and features that have been identified in the epic roadmap, makes sure that these contribute to the epic, and with that adds to the business value. The epic owner also identifies new business needs, capturing the Voice of the Customer and opportunities.

- The epic owner manages the epic roadmap and the associated investments, monitoring the business case.

- The epic owner manages risks, issues, and any other impediments that impact the delivery of the artifacts that have been agreed upon in the roadmap and the fulfillment of the epic. They support the product owners and managers in managing (business) priorities.

- Together with subject matter experts, architects, and business representatives, the epic owner defines the target product and the MVP, making sure that it matches with the Voice of the Customer, including all quality attributes.

- Shares the business vision and milestones with all stakeholders.

From the previous discussion, it should be clear that the epic owner must work closely together with the EA. But then what does the EA do? First, the EA is the sole owner of the business and technical architecture. With that, the EA drives the epic.

- The EA translates architecture strategy into epics.

- The EA defines the target business and technological architecture and sets the architecture principles to which epics, products, and features must comply.

- The EA defines and maintains technology standards, providing guidance on all architectural quality attributes, such as resilience, availability, security, observability, manageability, and consistency of build patterns.

- The EA must be consulted whenever a decision in delivery of epic roadmap artifacts leads to deviations of the standards. The EA advices on the impact and consequences of changes and informs the business leadership team.

- The EA is the linking pin between the business leaders and the business enablers.

So, the EA does become much more a strategist. But how does that rime with the servant leadership? First, the EA must be an excellent communicator, being able to talk both business and "tech." But there's one more skill that the EA must master: pragmatism. Unless the EA is involved in a startup and gets to build the architecture from the ground up, in most cases they will be confronted with an existing organization with a lot of technical debt. The role of the EA will be guiding the transformation, perhaps to something that looks like a startup.

Enterprises should never make that mistake, though. That mistake is trying to copy a startup. They can learn from startups, but they will never become one. Hence, EAs will almost never be in the position where they can start from scratch. The consequence of that is that the architecture will always be filled with compromises and a lot of pragmatic solutions. That doesn't mean that the EA shouldn't have the ambition to create a North Star as if it was developed from scratch. It means that building the roadmap toward that North Star might be frustrating from time to time where the compromise might be the best solution.

The most important role of the EA is being the bridge between business and technology, linking the business strategy with technology choices, defined in architectures and roadmaps. Next, the EA must be able to communicate about the link between business and technology, being able to translate complex material into comprehensive stories that all stakeholders can understand. Storytelling has become an important capability of the EA.

Let's summarize how the role of the EA will change:

- The EA will become more of an engineer. If there's one key takeaway from this book, then it's that the traditional EA will not fit the modern enterprise and the digital transformation. The modern enterprise is working in an agile way, embracing DevSecOps and likely be completely organized in a different way than the earth-born enterprise. The world of the enterprise is changing, customers are changing. Customers might not be looking for a specific product, but for an experience to which they can subscribe. Business models are changing rapidly. Innovation is the lifeline of the modern enterprise: it must continuously innovate and bring new experiences to the market at a much higher pace than in the predigital world. Let's make this very tangible: there's no time to spend months on ArchiMate diagrams. Teams must focus on getting MVPs out – minimal viable products – and start iterating from there. It means that the EA must start to think more like an engineer and be able to discuss with developers, programmers, and operations. Technical debt must be decommissioned, and new digital services launched and continuously improved in weekly, daily, or even hourly cycles. This requires a more hands-on mentality, also of the modern EA who must have deep knowledge and expertise of digital technology.

- The EA will become more of a coach. The EA has to come out of their ivory tower where they're spending their days studying TOGAF, Zachman, and scribbling in ArchiMate (no offense!), defining rules, guidelines, and guardrails that are implemented "top-down laws for doing architecture." The modern EA is part of the building and operating teams. The EA is still the guide, but more as a coach – the servant leader. The EA gets direct feedback from the teams and, more important, is closer to the Voice of the Customer. Together with the developers, the EA creates the solutions and supports the build of the MVP. Since the EA is now part of the team, they're also able to identify gaps and issues in a very timely manner, supporting in improving the way of working or in providing appropriate training. They're now guide, coach, and facilitator – not enforcing architecture, but enabling architecture.

- The EA will become more of a business strategist – engineer and coach, peer among peers, acting as the servant leader. Yet, the EA is still the linking pin between business and technology. The EA is involved in strategic business decisions, defining the North Star and developing the roadmaps describing how to get to that North Star.

You still want to become an EA? Congratulations. You have chosen to exercise one of the most exciting jobs in modern enterprises.

We need you.

Training New Talents: We Need You (Conclusion)

The world is changing. Enterprises are changing, because of the changes in the world. These might be small changes, but at time of writing, our world is in almost continuous state of shock with events that have a tremendous impact on all life on this planet. This book is not a political statement, nor does it seek to provide answers to global issues such as climate change, growing inequality, access to care, and the consequences of wars.

It all impacts our lives, and it impacts every single company. Companies must find ways to address issues, mitigate risks, and deal with impact of events that it can't influence. Companies need to be more agile than ever. Simple solutions do not exist. Cutting costs is not a sole answer to problems. Having a growth mindset, being business agile, and innovative is part of the answer. It's the only way to stay relevant as a business, despite all traditional advice that major consultancy firms still present in five sliders. Keep costs down and you will survive. The right advice is keep control of costs in operations, to create innovative power in development. It's a completely different ballgame.

This game requires a new type of players, as we have seen in this book. We need enterprise architects who really understand the new world of cloud and DevSecOps. Talents are hard to find: the war on talent is a fact in all industries and for almost every role. Just offering a lot of money to a talent isn't going to be the answer to attract hires. It's about the challenge and the right mindset of the enterprise: the growth mindset. Talents want to be able to have an impact.

But as we have seen already, the architect doesn't exist. Enterprises will likely end up with an enterprise architecture team, which is a good and recommendable direction. It allows enterprises to mix the experience of the traditionally trained EA with the new talents who focus on the digital transformation using agile, DevSecOps, cloud, and cloud native. It's going to be a mix of "things that have been done in the enterprise for good reasons" and "things that must be done in the enterprise for good reasons," to stay relevant in years to come.

Good EAs aren't trained in a day. They grow experience and expertise over the years, learning from the predecessors in the enterprise and at the same time work with the new building teams. The new EA seek fulfillment of their purpose. That purpose will inevitably be linked to the immense challenges that our world faces today and that enterprises need to address. To create solutions that fit that purpose, we need talents who understand both the heritage and the future, ready to lead to a more sustainable world through collaboration.

We need servant architecture leaders.

Summary

This chapter concludes this book about digital transformation and enabling this transformation through modern enterprise architecture. The role of the enterprise architect will change: the EA must step down from his ivory tower and become part of the developing and building teams. The EA still must have deep knowledge and expertise in business processes and technology, since they're the linking pin between the business and IT. Business models are changing and so is IT that is becoming more and more core activity of enterprise, instead of just an enabler. The EA must be able to explain new technology and how it's adding value to the business in comprehensive stories that every stakeholder can understand.

First and foremost, the EA must become an excellent communicator. Next, the modern EA is a true collaborator, working in teams as peer among peers, as the servant leader. The modern EA has an engineering mindset and is a coach and a business strategist.

It's a tough job, yet it's the most exciting job any enterprise has to offer in this age where any enterprise seeks to fulfill their new purpose in creating a better, sustainable world through digital technology. That's the true transformation.

Index

A

© Jeroen Mulder 2023
J. Mulder, *Modern Enterprise Architecture*, https://doi.org/10.1007/978-1-4842-9066-8

M

N